COMPOSING VIOLENCE

COMPOSING

Moyukh Chatterjee

A THEORY IN FORMS BOOK edited by Nancy Rose Hunt and Achille Mbembe

The Limits of Exposure

VIOLENCE

and the Making of Minorities

DUKE UNIVERSITY PRESS Durham and London 2023

Designed by Aimee C. Harrison
Typeset in Garamond Premier Pro and Avenir LT Std
by Westchester Publishing Services

Library of Congress Cataloging-in-Publication Data
Names: Chatterjee, Moyukh, [date] author.
Title: Composing violence : the limits of exposure and the making of
minorities / Moyukh Chatterjee.
Other titles: Theory in forms.
Description: Durham : Duke University Press, 2023. | Series: Theory in
forms | Includes bibliographical references and index.
Identifiers: LCCN 2022036266 (print)
LCCN 2022036267 (ebook)
ISBN 9781478017028 (hardcover)
ISBN 9781478019664 (paperback)
ISBN 9781478024293 (ebook)
Subjects: LCSH: Political violence—India—Religious aspects. | Ethnic
conflict—India. | Social conflict—India. | Religion and politics—India. |
Muslims—Violence against—India. | Minorities—Violence against—India. |
India—Politics and government. | BISAC: SOCIAL SCIENCE / Anthropology /
Cultural & Social | HISTORY / Asia / South / India
Classification: LCC HN690.Z9 V5 2023 (print) | LCC HN690.Z9 (ebook) |
DDC 303.60954—dc23/eng/20221117
LC record available at https://lccn.loc.gov/2022036266
LC ebook record available at https://lccn.loc.gov/2022036267

Cover art: Rummana Hussain, *Earth Picture*, 1993. Ink on cut acrylic,
terracotta, earth pigment and iron nails on board. Collection Kiran Nadar
Museum of Art, New Delhi, India. © Estate of Rummana Hussain.
Courtesy Talwar Gallery, New York | New Delhi.

In memory of Afroz Apa and Ram Narayan Kumar—
my companions on this journey

CONTENTS

ACKNOWLEDGMENTS

THIS BOOK is the culmination of a journey that started two decades ago. It is impossible for me to remember, let alone acknowledge, everyone in Delhi, Ahmedabad, Atlanta, Montreal, Bangalore, and Middlebury who have accompanied me on this journey. Over the last few years, I have relied on the kindness of a small circle of scholars: Saygun Gökariksel, Ram Natarajan, and Firat Bozcali have read most of the book. Pratiksha Baxi, Sahana Ghosh, and Thushara Hewage gave feedback during the final stretch. I had the good fortune of meeting with Ash Amin and Ravi Sundaram as I was discovering the heart of the book and their enthusiasm for the project was inspiring. Prathama Banerjee was kind enough to read the full manuscript and give generous feedback in the middle of a pandemic. I am grateful to her for encouragement that was essential for me to finish the manuscript. I am also grateful to Nancy Rose Hunt for helping the manuscript find a home.

At Azim Premji University, my wonderful colleagues at the School of Policy and Governance—Arun Thiruvengadam, Sitharamam Kakarala, Malini Bhattacharjee, Sudhir Krishnaswamy, Vishnupad, Sham Kashyap, Anshuman Singh, Kanika Gauba, Sambaiah Gundimeda, Sushmita Pati, Neeraj Grover, Prateeti Prasad, Sunayana Ganguly, and Siddhartha Swaminathan—gave valuable feedback during our beloved Thursday Seminar series. I am especially grateful to Ram, Sudhir, Malini, and Arun for their support in helping me find my feet in a new city with a two-year-old and a four-hour commute each day. Sunayana Ganguly made Bangalore feel like home and was always there to meet for a drink and go for a walk in Cubbon Park even when she had more exciting plans (which was always the case).

At McGill University, I am grateful to have met a warm and friendly group of scholars. Coffees and lunches with Megan Bradley, Manuel Balán, and Zinaida Miller were a welcome break from sitting at my desk in Peterson Hall. Fellow Postdocs at ISID and friends in Montreal—Katherine Bersch, S. P. Harish, Eric Hirsch, Poulami Roychowdhury, Brandon Hamilton, Nicole Rigillo, Catherine Larouche, Megha Sharma, and Andrew Ivaska—were wonderful companions. I want to especially thank Jimmy Lou and Sima Kokotovic for exploring Montreal with me. I am grateful to Katherine Lemons for supporting my postdoctoral application and giving feedback on my book proposal. Also at McGill, I had the opportunity to meet and learn from Erik Kuhonta, Francesco Amodio, Diana Allan, Kazue Takamura, Sonia Laszlo, Aruna Roy, Nikhil Dey, and Maitrayee Chaudhuri.

At Emory University, Bruce Knauft, David Nugent, and Gyan Pandey, were always willing to read yet another draft and meet me yet another time to discuss the seeds of the ideas in this book. Bruce Knauft, incredibly generous with his time and counsel, helped me navigate graduate school. David Nugent encouraged me to be curious about my fieldwork till the end and helped me explore the paradoxes of statecraft and power. Gyan Pandey's work on violence remains a touchstone for me, and it has inspired many of the questions I have asked in the book. I hope that the book contributes to the conversation around violence, minorities, majorities, and nationalism that Gyan's work opened for me as a graduate student in Delhi University. I also want to thank Geoff Bennington, Sander Gilman, Lynne Huffer, Cathy Caruth, Tom Flynn, Shoshana Felman, and Angelika Bammer for helping me to think outside my field. At Emory, I had wonderful peers—Sunandan, Durba Mitra, Navyug Gill, Ajit Chittambalam, Debjani Bhattacharjee, Sydney Silverstein, Pankhuree Dube, Shreyas Sreenath, Adeem Suhail, Shunyuan Zhang, Bisan Salhi, Sarah Franzen, Claire Marie Hefner, Swargajyoti Gohain, Aditya Pratap Deo, Guirdex Masse, Shatam Ray, and Anna Kurien. Shreyas Sreenath has been a guide for all things wise and wonderful, and his enthusiasm for the esoteric and eccentric has nourished my last stretch of writing. Sunandan's anarchism, dark humor, and fondness for theory helped me survive graduate school. Sebastián Dueñas's love for films has been a source of joy across time zones and continents.

At Middlebury, I want to thank friends who have nourished me with meals, conversations, and walks: Kristin Bright, Daniel Rosenblatt, Jenn

Ortegren, Ajay Verghese, Carly Thomsen, Nikolina Dobreva, Enrique Garcia, Laurie Essig, Daniel Houghton, Megan James, Caitlyn Ottinger, and Damien Arndt. And their wonderful children—Pepper, Zahi, Alex, Michelle, Vicky, Frankie, Joni, and Callum with whom I have spent so many joyous hours over the last three years. I want to especially thank Carly Thomsen for inviting me to a writing group that helped me stay on course and find a rhythm during the last few years of writing.

I had the pleasure of presenting parts of my book at the Law and Social Sciences Network (LaSSNet) at the University of Peradeniya, Delhi School of Economics, Krea University, Simon Fraser University, University of Ottawa, Bucknell University, Washington University, McGill University, University of Wisconsin Law School, University of Denver, Middlebury College, and Texas A&M University. I am grateful to the organizers and audiences at these places, especially Dinah Hannaford, Mayur Suresh, and Pratiksha Baxi for the invitation and support to present my work online and offline. I also benefited from presenting at the American Anthropological Association meetings and want to thank the co-organizers—Chelsey Kivland and Vibhuti Ramachandran—and discussants—Tobias Kelly, Sarah Muir, Ramah McKay, Sameena Mulla, Thom Blom Hansen, and Beatrice Jauregui. I want to thank the participants of the Harvard University Political Anthropology Working Group (PAWG)—especially Dilan Yildirim, Hayal Akarsu, Sahana Ghosh, and Xenia Cherkaev—where I received generous feedback on the introduction. I am grateful to the American Institute for Indian Studies (AIIS) and the organizers—Susan Wadley and Geraldine Forbes—and discussants—Rumela Sen, Hayden Kantor, and Radha Kumar—of the Book Workshop at the Madison South Asia Conference.

During moments of doubt, I have turned to friends who have not read the book but made sure through their words and actions that I could keep working on the manuscript. When my computer crashed, Dwaipayan Banerjee sent me his old computer (and I am writing these words on it since my computer has crashed again). Dwai has helped in too many ways for me to recount here: read my book proposal, shared his experience of publishing and writing multiple books, and always agreed to accompany me to the bookstore. I am lucky that I can always depend on Aditi Saraf's support and encouragement especially when things go downhill. Bharat Venkat helped me understand that the book never feels done and it was high time to let it go. I want to thank my teachers at the Department of Sociology, Delhi School of Economics, Deepak Mehta and Rita Brara, for their mentorship over the decades. I cannot imagine having begun this journey without their support. Over the years, I have also had the pleasure of discussing my work with Malvika Maheshwari, Madura Rasaratnam, P. Sanal Mohan, Farhana Ibrahim, Natasha Raheja, Vijayanka Nair, and Radhika Govindrajan.

If Delhi still feels like home, it is because of my friends—Ashis, Neetu, Sambuddha, Piyu, Uday, Swati, Samar, Lakshita, Sukhleen, Kunal, Swara, Prashant, Veda, and Akriti. Ashis, Prashant, and Swara will be most relieved that I have finished the book. I could not have finished the book without their friendship. Swara Bhaskar's passion for justice has accompanied me since our first trip to relief camps in Ahmedabad. Prashant Jha's love for all things political have helped me understand the big picture, even if I could not always put it down in writing. Ashis Roy's attention to the unthought but felt opened fields of inquiry and connections beyond the book. Also thanks to Ashis, I could finish my copyedits watching the mist roll through the mountains in Landour. Rahul Sarwate's passion for poetry and the history of ideas has been a source of great learning and he continues to inspire me to think and read beyond English.

In Gujarat, St. Xavier's College and the Behavioral Science Center hostel opened its doors to me in 2002, and I remember it as my home away from home. My first trip to Ahmedabad was with the Jagori Women's Resource Center. I want to thank the SARAI programme at CSDS, New Delhi, for an independent fellowship that helped me return to Ahmedabad in 2004. Ram Narayan Kumar, who passed away in 2009, was a model for a form of activism based on listening to survivors and introduced me to Harsh Mander and his team of extraordinary paralegals and lawyers at Nyayagraha. I want to acknowledge the generosity and friendship of Harsh and his team: Afroz Apa, Ishaaqbhai, Johanna, Prita, Mushtaqbhai, Muzaffarbhai, Altafbhai, Nasirbhai, Nazirbhai, Satishbhai, Chiragbhai, Usmanbhai, Umarbhai, Bhanubhai, Shareefa apa, and Shareefbhai. Afroz Apa, who passed away in 2016, accompanied me to relief colonies, introduced me to her friends, and shared her love for listening and telling stories. In Ahmedabad, I have had the privilege of learning from Ghanshyam Shah, Achyut Yagnik, Mukul Sinha, Gagan Sethi, Nupur Sinha, Father Cedric Prakash, Varsha Ganguly, Hiren Gandhi, Swaroop Dhruv, J. S. Bandukwala, Girish Patel, Sofia Khan, and Swati Joshi. I am thankful to Jayant J. Dabhi and Father Siddharth (and all my Gujarati teachers at Premal Jyoti) for helping me learn Gujarati. Renana Jhabvala and Janhavi Dave opened their houses to me for follow up fieldwork. I was fortunate to have to crossed paths with Johanna, Ankon,

Samantha, Bimal, Anumeha, Shahid, Hannah, Yuanjin, Niharika, Shardul, and Ganesh in Ahmedabad.

Parts of this book were published as articles in the *American Ethnologist, Law, Culture and Humanities*, and *Distinktion: Journal for Social Theory*. I want to thank the editors and anonymous reviewers of these journals for their feedback, especially Pablo Morales, Austin Sarat, and Niko Besnier. At Duke University Press, I want to thank my editor, Elizabeth Ault, for helping me to highlight the positive contribution of the book and for her support throughout the process, and Benjamin Kossak for helping me to prepare the manuscript for production. I am grateful to Catherine La Roche for formatting the manuscript. The fieldwork and writing of this book was made possible by the Wenner-Gren Dissertation Fieldwork Grant and the Hunt Postdoctoral Fellowship.

In Bangalore, Sandhya Iyengar, Indrajit Gupta, Usha Mukunda, Mukunda Mesho, Kumar Iyengar, Shashi, Michael, Kamala, Keerthi, and Shruthi have extended their care and warmth on numerous occasions. In Saket, Mamu, Mamia, Gops, Didi, and their families have always encouraged my writing. Evening walks with my mother in Lodhi Gardens, trips to the second-hand book market in Daryaganj with my brother, and reading the Sunday newspapers with my father are memories that I have carried with me across continents. My family in Delhi—Ilina, Mukul, and Kinshuk—have always listened to my arguments with indulgence, and I could not have finished the book without their unwavering support. If I was a poet, I would close this long song of thanks with an ode to my partner and son, Hemangini and Nikhil. During the last three years I have spent most of my time with my son. We went on long walks in the woods, spotted birds, noticed the seasons pass, listened to Otter Creek freezing and thawing, learned the names of wild-flowers, collected leaves, and painted sunsets. My other anchor, Hemangini Gupta, has used all her formidable talents to help me reach the end. She has read every word in this book, taken on extra work to financially support us, made plans to do fun things in new places, and listened to my endless list of complaints and transformed them into a neat list of things to do. Without her magical powers, I could not have finished this book.

APRIL 2002. Ahmedabad, the largest city in Gujarat in Western India. A cool early-morning breeze before the triumph of the blinding, burning summer sun. I stand in the parking lot of the Kalupur railway station, along with two friends, waiting to be picked up and taken to St. Xavier's College, where we will join volunteers pouring in from all parts of India to help victims of anti-Muslim riots. Since the end of March, we had seen mobs looting shops, burning tires, and brandishing daggers and sticks on television and in the newspapers. Scenes of what the mobs had left in their wake: corpses on the street, men and women standing like ghosts beside their charred houses, a plot of land full of bodies shrouded in white sheets, and families reduced to an eyewitness. Eventually, a man arrives to pick us up at the railway station, and we squeeze into an autorickshaw. Black holes—erstwhile shops, garages, and houses—pass us on both sides as we cross the Sabarmati River to enter the affluent western part of the city.

THE DESTRUCTION BY ITSELF WAS NOT SHOCKING. But I was unprepared to see the juxtaposition of mass destruction with mass pleasure. Smiling shopkeepers and customers inside unharmed shops stood beside gutted gaping holes in the streets. If I had a camera then, I would have made this photograph: two shops beside each other in a multilevel shopping mall, one of them a burned-out hole in the wall and the other a brightly lit square draped in fairy lights bustling with customers. I could touch, hear, and feel the violence by traveling to relief camps in the outskirts of the city where hundreds of Muslims slept under the open sky clutching bundles that contained everything they now possessed in the world (everything that was not burned or broken or disfigured or stolen by their neighbors). Or I could stop in the heart of the city, the tree-lined neighborhoods of the well-off Hindus and chat with anyone on the road, and I mean anyone at all. Like the jovial owner of a café, where I got my evening shot of special masala chai, who could barely contain his excitement at what had happened. *We finally taught them a lesson.*

The scene of the two shops that I saw on my first day in Gujarat was perhaps my first inkling that there was more to the scene of violence than horror and suffering. I would have to find a way of approaching violence beyond exposure. Why? Because there was no violence to "expose." The pogrom[1] had been televised. The police told Muslims: "We have no orders to save you,"[2] and Hindu mobs shouted slogans like "Yeh andar ki baat hai, police hamare saath hai" (This is an inside job, the police are on our side).[3] There was no public secret to reveal. Café owners, shopkeepers, and teachers freely expressed their satisfaction in teaching Gujarat's large Muslim minority community a lesson. Like the rest of India, Gujarat is majority Hindu, but it is also known as India's Hindu nationalist laboratory. A place where on your way to buy the Sunday papers you may pass a sign on the street urging you to take pride in being a Hindu; a place where an auto driver may ask you if you want to go to Hindustan (India) or Pakistan when you mention your destination is a Muslim-majority neighborhood.

The pogrom was on the surface of things: visible in posters and signs on the street, proclaimed at political rallies and speeches, and discussed in everyday conversations inside and outside the house. More than a decade after the pogrom, in 2016, I was sitting in the audience attending a World Cow Devotee's conference beside a young boy who revealed to me that he was learning to be a flutist. When we started talking and I said that I loved the sound of the flute, he asked me if I was a Hindu. When I said yes, he said that's why I was speaking to him so nicely. If you were a Muslim, you wouldn't mix with anyone. They like to be separate. He asked me if I knew about *Godhrakand* (the scandal at Godhra). You should have seen the way Hindus burned down Muslim homes. They entered their homes and burned them alive. After that you could roam the city like a lion. Since he was clearly too young to have witnessed the violence, I asked him how did he know all this? He told me he googled *Godhrakand* and watched videos, and his

I.1 "Say with Pride, We are Hindus," reads a billboard at a busy intersection in Ahmedabad in Gujarat, India. The billboard here was sponsored by the Hindu nationalist organization World Hindu Council (Viswa Hindu Parishad).

grammar teacher at school told him that when Muslim colonies were burning and if it appeared that the flames were dying, people on the street used their own petrol to rouse the fire. It was like a spring that had been pressed down for too long; when it's released, it can go anywhere.

On February 27, 2002, the Sabarmati Express arrived four hours late at Godhra in the western state of Gujarat. The train was filled with Hindu nationalists (*karsevaks*) who had gone to Ayodhya as part of a VHP (World Hindu Council) organized religious ceremony. Some of them argued and fought with the Muslim vendors at the railway station. They refused to pay for tea and snacks, made a failed attempt to abduct a young girl, forced at least one Muslim vendor to chant Hindu slogans, and tried to beat them up. A Muslim mob at the station started stoning the train.[4] Within fifteen minutes, a coach of the train had erupted in flames. By the time fire trucks arrived, fifty-nine Hindu men, women, and children were dead.

The VHP carried the charred bodies in a public procession across Ahmedabad, Gujarat's largest city. Local Gujarati newspapers printed photos of charred and disfigured bodies on their front pages with headlines like "Avenge Blood for Blood" and published false stories about Muslim mobs raping and cutting the breasts of Hindu women. The ruling Hindu nationalist government endorsed a widespread closure (*bandh*) of the entire state to protest the deaths of Hindus. During the shutdown, Hindu mobs burned, raped, and killed Muslims. Over one thousand people, mostly Muslims, were killed, while one hundred thousand were displaced. Scholarly, journalistic, and activist accounts of the violence have converged on a now well-documented fact: the Gujarat state government did not prevent the attacks on Muslims and even stoked anti-Muslim sentiment.[5] Even though the state government, led by Chief Minister Narendra Modi, was widely criticized for not stopping the violence, in 2014, Modi won a historic mandate to become India's new prime minister. In 2019, Modi was re-elected as prime minister surpassing his performance in 2014.

What work is possible when violence is *not* repressed, *not* located at the margins of the state, and *not* even disguised by the participants? What forms of legality, sociality, and politics transform spectacular violence into durable order? This book is an attempt at reading and writing violence beyond exposure by composing violence: tracing the forms of legality that make the witness a malicious and unreliable minority; reading archives of violence where patterns of destruction intersect with patterns of intimacy; noting the circulation, dispersal, and proliferation of sexual violence as constitutive of minoritization; and thus making a map that shows how and why political violence plays a key role in the making and maintenance of modern states based on majorities and minorities.

Since 2002, I have been visiting Gujarat, first as a volunteer working in relief camps for Muslim survivors and then as an anthropologist. Over the last decade, I have tracked the afterlives of the violence:[6] sitting with witnesses in the courtroom; accompanying paralegals as they visited survivors and updated them about their legal cases; listening to human rights activists talk to witnesses about what, where, when, and how they saw what they saw; watching angry debates between activists and lawyers as their cases collapsed in the courtroom; and accompanying filmmakers, students, artists, and journalists who came to Gujarat to document the horror.

As India's first televised pogrom, the violence in Gujarat received unprecedented media and activist attention. Investigative reports and secret tapes showed men boasting about raping and murdering Muslims;[7] newspaper editorials and opinion pieces announced the death of Indian secularism; the Supreme Court of India compared the government to "modern day Neros" who looked elsewhere "when innocent women and children were burning." The scenes from the massacre kept changing—the indescribable torture of women and the pleasure of the men who bragged about it, survivors cooking and sleeping in relief camps ankle deep in sewage, pamphlets that asked Hindus to "give the traitorous Muslims a taste of patriotism by boycotting them socially and economically,"[8] police refusing to register complaints against Hindus—but the frame of analysis remained the same: *exposing the exceptional*. Exposing—state violence, sexual violence, partisan police, bigoted politicians, illegality, impunity, the silence of intellectuals, the rumors of the press. Exceptional—suffering, brutality, terror, horror, breakdown of law and order, the failure of the state, the death of secularism, the collapse of civil society.[9]

I noticed that our response to political violence against minorities continues to treat it as either exceptional (by calling it a genocide) or instrumental (by focusing on political actors fomenting violence for electoral gains). Even perspectives that approach violence from opposite ends of the political spectrum (the left and the right) deal with a familiar cast of characters—partisan police, unscrupulous politicians, and rioting mobs. And familiar objects of analysis—the deadly ethnic riot, the poisonous ideology of communalism, the deep cultural roots of Hindu nationalism, the weak postcolonial state, and its brittle rule of law.

Ultimately, this mise-en-scène frames political violence within a familiar problem-space[10] that entails a mode of analysis I call the *politics of exposure*: exposing the partisan state, biased police and politicians, and the failure of the rule of law. A problem-space, Scott elaborates, is an "ensemble of questions and answers around which a horizon of identifiable stakes (conceptual as well as ideological-political stakes) hangs."[11] In this sense, the politics of exposure is a mode of reading and writing violence that flows through both academic and nonacademic work. One can find its traces in investigative journalism and activist writing but also in political theory and scholarly work that seeks to expose violence.[12]

This book argues that the politics of exposure is inadequate to understand violence against minorities within liberal democracies. First, the politics of exposure assumes that violence is hidden across cultural contexts and, once exposed, will invite predictable effects (justice) and positive affects (like condemnation and empathy). Second, the exposure model predominantly works with concepts like erasure and repression that do not help us understand the productive life of violence within democracies—the procedures and techniques immanent to the rule of law, the making of news, and archives that produce majorities and minorities. Third, the politics of exposure does not reflect on the paradoxes entailed in acts of exposure—like reproducing the modes of address and affects that frame the object that one is seeking to unveil in the first place. Finally, the politics of exposure exceptionalizes political violence as a peculiar pathology of societies in the Global South. This gesture risks setting up an imaginary normative democracy elsewhere (usually understood to be somewhere in North America or Western Europe)[13] and obstructs our understanding of the place of political violence within democracies across the Global North and South. The politics of exposure is like taking a well-trod path in the aftermath of political violence. It is familiar, even comforting; it takes us to a place where we see terror and suffering, victims and perpetrators, and it satisfies our desire to unveil hidden actors and conspiracies with the clarity of anger and moral outrage. And yet this comforting attitude may not be adequate to our present moment because far-right movements across the world are based on forms of violence that are fundamentally transformational and productive, public and collective, illegal but licit, often sanctioned by the state, and foundational to the making of "the people."

To be clear, I have experienced the pleasures and disappointments of exposure and can hardly speak of completely abandoning it, insofar as it would mean that I abandon the ground on which this project started. The politics of exposure is part of my journey. I have worked alongside human rights activists and paralegals and lawyers who are invested in the politics of exposure and that it was no doubt the politics of exposure in the form of newspaper editorials, human rights reports, and investigative journalism that produced the feelings of outrage and anger that set me on the path to understanding the significance of public violence against minorities in India. Exposure has immediate and important effects: it sparks into being new publics and produces affects that motivate actions and feelings for justice and truth beyond the scene of violence. So, what I am proposing is not an abandonment of exposure but a side-stepping, walking around it when there is nothing to unmask.[14]

Given the limits of exposure, how do we approach public and collective forms of antiminority violence? There are several ways to avoid, exceed, and work beside exposure. One approach is to acknowledge that liberalism as a loose bundle of ideas, practices, and attachments has always coexisted with institutional and unofficial violence against minorities. And at different points in time across world areas, the authority of the violent mob has happily coexisted with the rule of law.[15] In other words, the ability to kill and punish, the heart of sovereign power, is deployed not only by state actors like the police but also nonstate actors like local "big men" and political activists and organizations. Another route to think about violence beyond exception begins with a reexamination of the everyday and the routine. Taking this path means tracking the tentacles of violent events within everyday social life and exploring the histories, archives, and languages that mask the exceptional as routine.[16] Violence viewed through this lens appears less as a breakdown and more as a continuation of social ties and political arrangements.

None of these paths are isolated from each other, and I imagine them less as forks in the road and more as trails in the forest that crisscross each other, weaving in and out, running parallel to my own path.[17] At the beginning, however, I abandon the framework of norm-exception that characterizes normative political theory's approach to postcolonial politics.[18] More specifically, the foundation of Western states like the United States and Canada on the expulsion and subjugation of Indigenous and Black people, and contemporary violence against these communities in Western liberal democracies, is a reminder that violence against minorities is not a deviation from modernity but an integral aspect of the making of the modern nation-state itself. If mass political violence against minorities plays a key role in the making of the nation-state, then forms of collective violence like pogroms can help us understand the production and reproduction of permanent majorities and minorities within modern nation-states.[19] Pogroms are attempts to constitute a society based on what B. R. Ambedkar called a "permanent majority." Ambedkar made a crucial distinction between a political majority, which is "always made, unmade and remade," and a "permanent majority," which is fixed and immutable.[20] This book maps the power of violence to create permanent majorities and minorities.

From Exposure to Composition

I suggest that one way of working beyond the politics of exposure is to compose violence. This means giving an account of violence not as a dark object that will wither in the light of critique but as a force that flows through spaces and bodies creating new attachments and feelings, new subjects and subjectivities. Take, for instance, my initial example of the photograph that I wish I had composed when I first arrived in Ahmedabad, a photograph that would show the juxtaposition of pain and pleasure, the distant and the intimate,[21] the destructive and the productive in the same frame and, in doing so, show the afterlife of a pogrom that is not a public secret but is worn on the sleeve of a regime and a people as a matter of pride. To make up for that lost opportunity, in these pages, I compose what to my mind are objects that keep recurring in discussions of political violence—event, archive, witness, the rule of law, the unspeakable, and justice. I look at police reports that do not erase mass violence against Muslims but aggregate different instances or arson and destruction into a single report that attributes the violence to colonial racial categories of "communal mobs"; a form of police writing to keep violence visible yet unaccountable; police writing that makes connections with a supremacist social order being forged outside the archive; legal trials that use the survivors' testimonies to transform them into malicious sectarian subjects who are falsely accusing Hindus; and anti-impunity activism that in trying to expose state violence through proceduralism ends up reinforcing the second-class status of Muslims in a Hindu-dominated society.

This approach is different from trying to represent the unrepresentable, speak the unspeakable, and unveil the dark, deep world of hidden violence. To compose violence, then, is to show how violence persists, motivates, and animates social and political life beyond the scene of horror. To compose is to take on board Walter Benjamin's distinction between law-preserving and law-making violence,[22] and move away from the idea that violence is always a breakdown, interruption, and exception. Instead, a compositional account gives us a sense of how violence stitches together new scenes, bodies, and spaces[23] to create a majority and minority population. To compose violence is to describe violence as a constitutive force that produces and reproduces the permanent majority and the minority—on the street, in the courtroom, and in the police archive.

Composition requires a way of touching, feeling, reading, and writing violence[24] that moves away from what Saidiya Hartman calls ritual invocations of the "shocking and the terrible."[25] And to ask, "And what virtue remains in the act of unmasking when we know fully well what lies beneath the mask?"[26] In situations where violence is on the surface of police reports, courtroom proceedings, legal judgments, newspaper reports, and mainstream media, then scholarly work cannot sequester itself from concerns that are addressed more squarely in the realm of art. J. M. Coetzee argues that novelists writing about torture confront a challenge: "how not to play by the rules of the state, how to establish one's own authority, how to imagine torture and death on one's own terms."[27] I feel that this challenge of writing violence in a new key is not solely a novelist's burden but a question about form that confronts anyone who wants to do more than simply expose violence. If form is understood as "an arrangement of elements—an ordering, patterning, or shaping,"[28] then specific forms of violence produce their own configurations of time, space, body, and affect.

Consider the pogrom: mobs, police, and ordinary people kill, loot, and attack minorities with impunity. Men with swords and sticks dance on the streets beside burning shops and bodies. If we focus on exposure, we risk overlooking the pogrom as a public spectacle, as a technique to make the insider outsider.

What kind of belonging is produced during massacres when the government of the day shuts down the city so that ordinary people may participate in the public punishment of Muslims? And how is this violence reproduced over time and across sites—in the police archive and police station, inside the courtroom, at home, in the offices of NGOs, and in the everyday lives of victims and perpetrators, who are also neighbors and survivors. To ask such questions helps us to understand the role of pogroms in state formation and the making of "the people," which is inseparable from the making of the majority/minority.

To examine the long arc of violence, I turn to police paperwork that inscribe pogroms as ethnic violence, forms of media that reproduce the colonial logic of ancient racial hatred, and forms of legality that are techniques to create and govern a social order divided into the "minority" (Muslim) and the "majority" (Hindu). By paying attention to these forms and feelings that often lie on the surface of police documents, courtroom proceedings, human rights activism, and media, I show how violence is a force that is used by a range of actors to forge new scenes that brings together new sets of actors, materials, and affects.

In my efforts to compose violence, I have been inspired by recent debates in literary studies and critical theory around the limits of critique, which for me also reads as the limits of exposure. I was struck by the key role of "violence" within these debates. Take this sentence from Eve Sedgwick's now classic essay on paranoid and reparative reading: "Why bother exposing the ruses of power in a country where, at any given moment, 40 percent of young Black men are enmeshed in the penal system?"[29] I read this as an example of the limits of "exposing" anti-Black violence and racism, which pervades American society; the limits of the idea that anti-Black violence is a hidden aspect of an otherwise liberal democracy. In the same essay, Sedgwick develops her influential concept of reparative reading, which is a form of critical work based on love and amelioration rather than suspicion and exposure. The fact that Sedgwick's push toward reparative reading is worked out through the public knowledge of structural anti-Blackness—the mass incarceration of Black people in the United States—tells us that the object violence plays a pivotal role in instigating a search for new forms of reading and writing. Similarly, the influential call for "surface reading" uses the example of torture to express its frustration with an older symptomatic method of interpretation that focuses on unveiling hidden meanings underneath the text. "Those of us who cut our teeth on deconstruction, ideology, critique, and the hermeneutics of suspicion have often found those demystifying protocols superfluous in an era when images of torture at Abu Ghraib and elsewhere are immediately circulated on the internet."[30] In both reparative and surface reading, I detect an exhaustion with the politics of exposure, and in this sense, they are paths that run along the one I sketch out in this book.

In a similar vein, Bruno Latour offers compositionism as an alternative to critique, insofar as it underlies that "things have to be put together (Latin *componere*) while retaining their heterogeneity."[31] For Latour, composition helps us move away from the "irrelevant difference between what is constructed and what is not constructed, toward the crucial difference between what is *well* or *badly* constructed, *well* or *badly* composed."[32] Composition, in this sense, is a practical question, a question of choosing the right tool for the right situation because "it is no more possible to compose with the paraphernalia of critique that it is to cook with a seesaw."[33]

The impulse to compose violence begins by acknowledging that the covers are off: there is no shame, no guilt, and thus the toolkit of exposure comprising terms like silencing, erasure, and repression can feel like cooking with a seesaw. Instead, there is an atmosphere of public and festive violence. To compose such scenes is to make a map where violence is not a hidden spot marked X that lies behind locked doors but is instead a force that motivates, persists, and animates. In this sense, this book is not so much about defining what is violence, or whether to call what happened in Gujarat a pogrom, riot, genocide, or massacre, but rather: how does it persist, and what does it have going for it?[34] By focusing on the surface, on what is repeated, aggregated, circulated, and distributed and thus flourishes in conditions of visibility, I try to forge an ethnographic approach to violence that does not assume it is always already invisible, erased, and repressed. And neither is it a place of return, the universal ground to feel a common humanity with others based on suffering and pain.[35]

Instead, I focus on the transformational quality of political violence. I follow the pogrom as it is debated in the courtroom, inscribed in police reports, framed by activists as state impunity, and disseminated in the media as ethnic violence—producing and reproducing the majority and the minority. Put differently, I focus on how Muslims become malicious and unreliable witnesses in the courtroom, how the police inscribe anti-Muslim attacks as a war between Hindus and Muslims, how the judge transforms rioting Hindus into passive bystanders, and how the spectacles of the pogrom become blank documents in the police archive. These enduring effects of violence suggest that violence against minorities is better understood as a catalyst. In fact, the transformations brought about by political violence against minorities (the violence is both targeted at minorities and plays an important role in making them minorities) is integral to both the making and maintenance of the modern nation-state and the performance of democracy itself. In trying to link the productive life of antiminority violence to the performance of the law and the making of the public, I focus on how particular forms of violence are "intrinsic to the production of liberal democracy in which state actors simulate social actors and social actors bring into play quasi-state categories and practices in order to maintain representational continuity across the formal state-society division."[36] By highlighting legality, archives, media, and activism that give meaning, value, and significance to the core of democratic politics like majority, minority, the state, and the people, impunity is not the perversion of democracy but is intrinsic to the performance of liberal democracy based on its logic of number and majoritarianism.[37]

Scholars of violence contend that postcolonial sovereignty and statecraft is based on the "subjugation of life to the power of death,"[38] exhibiting a theatrical and dramaturgical mode of power,[39] proliferating techniques of violence including disappearance, torture, and secrecy.[40] Building on this rich body of work that highlights the continuity between war and peace, rationality and violence, order and disorder, this book grapples with legality, archives, and procedures that transform ongoing violence against minorities into durable forms of democratic rule. This transformation is key in contexts across the Global South and North where the necropolitical project[41] is championed by the state and nonstate actors attack, subjugate, and intimidate minorities as a matter of pride. Put differently, across contexts, whether it is the Rohingyas in Myanmar or Kurds in Turkey or Palestinians in Israel and Gaza, violence against minorities as a mode of people and state making is now hyper-visible across many world contexts. This ongoing minoritization is based on affects, temporalities, and techniques that proliferate and absorb violence in modern states to constitute the political. The political, here, is understood as the process by which modern states absorb, capture, and frame violence to secure, consolidate, and invent forms of dualistic rule based on majorities and minorities. This is the deep political work done by antiminority violence insofar as it touches the very ground on which nation-states stand and endure.

What is the space of the minor and the minority within modernity? Juxtaposing the Jewish question in Europe with the Muslim question in India, Aamir Mufti argues that "the terrorized and terrifying figures of minority"[42] are at the heart of the crisis of modern secularism and liberalism. The "repeated explosions of intolerance in American history," Talal Asad writes, "are entirely compatible (indeed intertwined) with secularism in a highly modern society."[43] This perspective frames the question of violence against minorities as wholly modern and foundational to modern ideas of nationalism, liberalism, and secularism. In other words, the truly extraordinary quality about the public murders of Muslims on the streets of India and the transformation of India into a de facto Hindu State is the compatibility of anti-Muslim violence with the everyday functioning of a modern secular state and its rule of the law.[44] Even though all minorities occupy a vulnerable position within modern states, there is something about a certain kind of minority—whether Jews in Europe or Muslims in India and Europe—that brings to fore the anxiety of who really belongs to the nation-state. This is linked to the two contradictory conceptions of belonging, the cultural/popular (the nation) and the constitutional/legal (the state),[45] that reside inside the concept of the nation-state. This creates an "irresolvable tension" at the heart of the concept of the minority. On the one hand, "a minority is supposed to be an equal partner in the building of the nation; on the other hand, its difference (religious, racial, ethnic) poses an incipient threat to the identity of the nation that is grounded in the religious, linguistic, and cultural norms of the majority."[46]

While there may be many ways to resolve this tension, riots, pogroms, gas chambers, lynching, displacement, and dispossession shadow minorities, especially those perceived to pose an existential threat to the "mainstream of the natural political community"[47] that constitutes the nation-state. In this sense, the minor and minorities are a permanent critique of the dominant and the normative since they bring to fore the unresolved question of difference and its politicization.[48] Minorities, even as they are supposed to be a part of the national, contain within them differences that can unravel the fantasies of the majoritarian machine within modern states.

This larger question casts its shadow on the Indian attempt to settle the minority question through displacement, riots, pogroms, and lynching and its relationship with processes of minoritization in other parts of the world. Talal Asad has argued that the status of Muslims and Islam in Europe is a good place to understand the effects of the myth of Europe as a homogenous space within which Muslims become a minority who must shed their religious symbols and practices before they can be tolerated and assimilated. Asad argues that "it is precisely because Muslims are external to the essence of Europe that 'coexistence' can be envisaged between 'us' and 'them.'"[49] This idea of us versus them is possible only when we consider what Asad calls the "cultural idea of a minority," which is not quantitative but refers to the creation of a group, a community, outside the culture of "the People" (nation) who stand in for "the majority." Minorities may be inside the state (and enjoy all the privileges that come with formal citizenship) and yet be outside the culture.[50] This idea makes sense only within the modern conception of the nation-state where each people has a singular culture, identity, religion, and language.

There is then an enduring tension between the imagined abstract individual of liberal democracy (the vision defended by human rights activists), political rule based on "number,"[51] and the minority as a cultural group that is defined by its difference from the majority.[52] This tension imperils minorities who are considered an impediment to the nation's attempts to unify and homogenize a territory under one flag, one religion, and one culture. Any group classified and perceived by the state and the people as a minority is always available for violence in the name of nationalism and the will of the majority. Nationalism, in this sense, "continuously constructs social and political hierarchies, privileged languages, and relations of dominance and subordination, not only outside but *within* the natural modern political community and state."[53]

Can a book that so explicitly revolves around violence against minorities take up the minor as something more than subjection and abjection? Since the overall aim of the book is to compose violence, I turn to the minor not as a quantitative category, or even a site for social suffering, but a way of reading the scene of violence and its afterlives. To track the formation and circulation of violence in mainstream media, and its patterning in police archives as a lens to understand the limits of human rights activism and the law itself, and finally to understand the production of the "Hindu" and "Muslim" not as fixed categories but as sliding signifiers that are given a meaning and significance in the present.[54]

To do so, I derive minor concepts—repetition, aggregation, exaggeration, distribution, and circulation—that absorb, sustain, and proliferate violence. The minor can be the vantage point to understand the artificiality of the major. It is the minor incident that triggers the "communal riot" but remains unexplained in mainstream media, the minor name (alias) that is used by judges and lawyers in the courtroom to dismiss testimony. The minor is also the atmosphere in the courtroom, the endless waiting that exhausts witnesses to the point that they begin to lose faith in those who are trying to help them; and it is often the minor characters in mainstream media that interrupt the seamless narrative of majorities versus minorities. The minor is like a little thread that, if you pull for long enough, may unspool the stability of the major. All this is to say that to follow the minor is to compose violence in ways that allow us to see what was always visible differently. In this book, it gives us a sense of how minorities and majorities are produced and reproduced, and how that is inseparable from a wider political struggle to define the terms of belonging and citizenship within liberal-democratic regimes.

JULY 2008. I reach Ahmedabad on the first day of the Rath Yatra, the mega Hindu religious procession that courses through the narrow veins of the old city at glacial speed accompanied by elephants, drummers, and song. I want to see the procession, but friends warn me against going. "There's always some trouble, especially when they pass Muslim neighborhoods." "You'll be waiting for hours and still miss it because of the crowds." I pick up my camera and backpack and still go to see it. I see a river of young men, flanked by drummers, elephants adorned with colorful jackets, priests showering flowers at spectators, and little kids picking up the flotsam and jetsam that trails the procession. I find a corner from where I think I have a good vantage point to photograph the idols and the procession. In the balconies around me, windows are open, and men, women, and children are peering out to catch a glimpse of the gods. The terraces are packed with kids.

Suddenly, I feel someone tugging at my backpack and instinctively grab it. I notice that two men have created a small ripple in what was earlier a moving body of people. Two policemen. One is significantly younger than the other; he's the junior one, clean shaven, wearing tight-fitting trousers and shiny schoolboy black shoes; he's the one who does all the shoving and pushing, while the older presumably senior policeman stands behind him asking questions. The questions come so fast I feel like I am drowning in them. I barely notice that the younger one has taken off my backpack and is examining my camera as I try to answer their questions.

What's your name? Why are you here? What's in your bag? What's inside your pockets?

I am a student . . . just came to see the procession . . .

The people in the crowd start arranging themselves around me in the shape of a ring, and I can feel eyes all over me. I am no longer a spectator. I am the spectacle. I see amused faces, faces with the holy mark on the forehead, tonsured heads, and men standing with their arms linked together. I am the only one with a beard. The younger policeman empties the contents of my bag on the street. I make some weak noises of protest. There is laughter in the background. The older policeman is flipping through my field notes and is holding my wallet in the other hand. They read the name of a hotel where I was sitting with a human rights team a few hours ago.

Who were you meeting in Epsilon hotel? What train did you take to come to Ahmedabad? From where?

My heart is racing even though I have done nothing wrong. My field notes feel like contraband, full of words like impunity, illegal, police firing, riots. . . . I am secretly praying that they don't find the copy of a citizen's inquiry report on the 2002 riots. "Now take a picture with your camera in front of us." I point my Nikon FE10 at the burning blue sky and hear the click. "What were you doing at the hotel?" The whole thing ends as suddenly as it started when they discover my father's visiting card in my wallet. "What's this?" I tell them that he works for the Central government in Delhi.

I.2
A public sign in Ahmedabad that displays the phone number and directions to the Paldi branch of the Bajrang Dal, a youth-based Hindu nationalist organization.

Inside the Laboratory of Hindu Nationalism

In December 2002, the president of the World Hindu Council (VHP), Pravin Togadia, described the pogrom as a successful experiment in the "laboratory of *Hindutva*"—a label that has since been used in popular and scholarly writing to describe the western state of Gujarat. Hindutva, also called Hindu nationalism, is a Hindu supremacist ideology that casts religious minorities, especially Muslims in India, as outsiders. Gujarat was only the beginning. "We will make a laboratory of the whole country. This is our promise and resolve," Togadia declared at a press conference covered by the *Hindustan Times* on December 16, 2002. The political and social movement—Hindu nationalism—is an all-India phenomenon that is often traced to the establishment of the RSS (National Volunteer Corp) in 1925. Its intellectual roots can be traced to the simultaneous racialization and minoritization of Muslims during British colonial rule. Not only did colonial rule emphasize religious difference as a lens to understand and govern India but it also created stereotypes of the meek and effete Hindu versus the hostile and rebellious Muslim. These images are strewn throughout the writings of Hindu nationalists. Savarkar wrote an essay titled "The Essentials of Hindutva" in 1923 in which he sought to define the meaning of what it means to be a Hindu through its opposition to the Muslim as an invader and despot. Since then, the movement has transformed into a conglomerate of different organizations, ideologically and politically linked to each other, popularly called the *Sangh Parivar* (Family of Hindu-Nationalist Organizations) with the common aim of uniting Hindus and transforming India into a *Hindu Rashtra* (Hindu Nation). The Hindu nationalist "family" includes the "founding" RSS (volunteer-based organization that runs schools, hospitals, and performs charitable works), the VHP that maintains ties with nonresident Indian (NRI) Hindus and promotes Hindu religious values, and the political party BJP (which was known as the second-largest party in India after the Congress but is now the dominant political force in most parts of India). Apart from these major organizations, there are cadre-based organizations like the youth-based group *Bajrang Dal* and an exclusively women's wing called *Durga Vahini*. Gujarat 2002 did not end with mob violence against Muslims; it was the beginning of a process that would attempt to create a society based on the idea of Muslims as permanent second-class citizens, and this idea was now electorally successful and publicly acceptable in at least one part of the country.

One of my first memories of visiting Ahmedabad was a person telling me to go back to "Pakistan" when they saw me walk out of a Muslim-majority neighborhood. On another occasion, a young man sitting next to me at a cow protection event told me with a straight face about the razor-sharp invisible wires that sliced the hands and necks of Hindus who strayed into the old parts of the city. Once during dinner, when I asked my landlady in Ahmedabad if her children had Muslim friends, she smiled and said that "we [Hindus] are different from them, and we just don't get along with them [Muslims]."

A flurry of articles written by eminent Gujarati historians and intellectuals sought to provide context and meaning to a shocking event: Why Gujarat? Was Gujarat an extreme case of forces brewing all over the country, or was it something altogether different? Gandhi's legacy loomed large over these questions. Gandhi, the apostle of nonviolence, the spirit of the anticolonial movement, and a lifelong warrior for Hindu-Muslim amity. Gandhi was born in Gujarat and had set up his first ashram on the banks of the Sabarmati.

At the heart of these questions is the metaphor of Gujarat as a laboratory for Hindu supremacy that far exceed its borders insofar as the pogrom initiated a wider process of constructing a certain kind of Hindu and Muslim. In other words, what ideas about the self, society, and statecraft allowed Gujarat to become a laboratory for Hindu supremacy? To answer this question, I turn to ideas in Gujarat about who belongs and who does not; a history of the idea of Muslims as outsiders; a history of violence that shows that public protests and caste violence in Ahmedabad often transformed into attacks against Muslims; and the rise of Gujarati *Asmita* (Pride) that labels all critique as an impediment to development and success.[55] Togadia's confidence that the experiment in Gujarat could be replicated across India was based on the idea that the pogrom was part of a long-standing project in the creation of India as a Hindu nation.[56]

Hindu nationalists were influenced by colonial British accounts such as A. K. Forbes's *Ras Mala: Hindoo Annals of the Province of Gooserat in Western India (1856)*, which on page one describes Hindus as the "race whose rule was supplanted by that of the crescent" and the history of Gujarat as an elegy to the splendor and glory of a time before the "avalanche of Mohummedan invasion."[57] Forbes also described the "tall minaret of the Moslem" in Ahmedabad as a symbol of Muslim tyranny.[58] This mode of writing history was adopted by Gujarati scholars in the nineteenth century who started dividing the past according to the religious membership of the ruler, a colonial historiography was not limited to Gujarat or for that matter professional historians. This colonial history of Hindus as a race defeated by invading Muslims cemented the idea that "the true history of India was five thousand years long, and that the Muslims in India were foreigners, whose only relation to the native inhabitants was one of despotism."[59]

Once the past was divided into Hindu, Muslim, and British periods, then the decline of the glory of the Hindu period was directly related to the arrival of outsiders—the Muslims and then the British. This colonial narrative gained prominence even though alternative strands in nineteenth-century accounts of the region emphasized the flourishing of trade and commerce under Muslim rulers.[60] The idea that Muslims were outsiders and invaders, coauthored by colonial and native historians, was based on the image of the weak and tolerant Hindu, who was overrun and dominated by aggressive invaders.

This idea of the weak, effeminate, and vegetarian Gujarati Hindu overrun by strong, hypermasculine meat-eating Muslims motivated Hindu rioters during the pogrom to perform brutal forms of violence against Muslim women to secure their masculinity. Hindu rioters said they felt like martial historical figures like Maharana Pratap when they raped Muslims and galvanized their low-caste identity (as meat eaters who could answer Muslims in their own coin).[61]

Gujarat as a laboratory for Hindu supremacy may seem scandalous, since it suggests the complete repudiation of Gandhian values of tolerance and nonviolence. But even as Gandhi pioneered civil disobedience and nonco-operation tactics against the British in Gujarat, his influence was not limited to ideas of nonviolence. The Gandhian influence on Gujarati public culture is equivocal. According to Howard Spodek, Gandhian influence had a dou-ble edge, and in the 1980s, the nonviolent aspect of his politics had faded away, even as a "certain level of violence in political protest activity had be-come acceptable and even normative."[62] In Ahmedabad, violent agitations and protests became the norm. The expression of public violence as dissent "illuminated a tragic irony of the Gandhian legacy. Part of Mahatma's (Gan-dhi) message had been an emphasis on non-violence; another element was militant protest for social, economic, and political enfranchisement."[63] In other words, Gandhi's impact on Hindu-Muslim relations in Gujarat was not a settled question. And it kept coming up during my fieldwork.

At one meeting, I heard a group of visiting human rights activists ask the well-known civil rights advocate Girish Patel, "How could this hap-pen in Gandhi's land?" Patel responded by saying that "the people, and the middle-class, never supported Gandhi in his own birthplace. They thought he was pro-Pakistan, pro-minorities. Only those who don't know our his-tory will be surprised that this [pogrom] happened here." Patel was echoing a point many scholars familiar with Gujarat's history have made before. Ashis Nandy wrote that "Gujarat disowned Mohandas Karamchand Gandhi long ago"[64] and that the middle class were representative of a larger politi-cal trend in Gujarat that had forsaken Gandhian values of religious amity. Gandhian scholar Tridip Suhrud wrote that "Gandhi's absence is nowhere more palpable than in present-day Gujarat."[65]

Like the nineteenth-century Gujarati intellectuals who described the Muslim period as a fall from the glory of the Hindu period, it is easy to fall into the trap of writing a history of Gujarat as a story of its decline from premodern tolerance to modern fanaticism, from Gandhi's land to Toga-dia's laboratory, from peace-loving merchants to far-right fanatics. Such an account focusing as it does on Gujarat as an aberration misses the wider construction of Muslims as outsiders in the making of India.[66] In Gujarat, a general conservativism, the lack of a robust trade union movement, and the absence of a Dalit anticaste politics allowed the process of Hindu na-tionalism to proceed without any impediments.[67] The absence of progres-sive social movements meant that there was a lack of a public culture that would critique dominant conceptions of development, caste, and religion. Additionally, there was a shift in the 1960s in what Ghanshyam Shah calls "the style of politics."[68] This "transformation from elitist to mass politics" meant that "vague Gandhian concepts of propriety" that emphasized accommodation were replaced by the politics of coercion and intimidation. Even when this politics of intimidation was not directed against Muslims, confrontations between students and the government transformed into "communal riots."

Take, for example, the massive student agitation in 1974. Initially these oppositional, student-led movements were directed against the corrupt government of the day. But these movements were also marked by the active participation of Hindu nationalist groups like the Jan Sangh (the organization that later became the official political party, the BJP). In these agitations against police atrocity, price rise, and corruption, "there was no inhibition as regards violence."[69] Decades before Gujarat 2002, student leaders "advocated violence in public" and made public speeches announcing that they would no longer follow Gandhian nonviolence. It was also during this time that Hindu nationalists started to win elections and gain ground in local politics. This rise of the BJP (the political wing of the Hindu nationalists) was mirrored by the slow demise and eventual decimation of the Indian National Congress, the dominant political party till the 1980s that had built a winning coalition of the state's lower castes, religious minorities, and tribals. Like the student agitations in the 1970s, protests against affirmative action policies for lower castes transformed into communal riots in 1985 in Ahmedabad. The entanglement of anti-Muslim violence with popular politics in Gujarat helps us understand not so much the unbroken history of antagonism between Hindus and Muslims, but the transformation of class and caste differences within Hindu society into violence against Muslims.[70]

The conditions of possibility for anti-Muslim violence in Gujarat are also based on the patronage and political infrastructure that circulated political goods and services. In fact, "as wide-ranging networks of various brokers and intermediaries have formed to facilitate the interaction between state institutions and ordinary citizens, politicians have acquired the necessary local authority, contacts and incentives to foment violence."[71] The participation of Hindu nationalist organizations in relief work after floods and earthquakes accounts for their robust presence in neighborhood-level politics.[72] What Gujarat shows, then, is a culmination of multiple streams of politics, culture, and history that over time produce a publicly acknowledged and politically sustainable form of Hindu supremacy. The Gujarat experiment can be replicated in any modern state where the wider public accepts the idea that an invasive minority lives inside the space of the majority, who are a different species from them, forever estranged, forever at war with them.

Composing the Legal

Gafar, a Muslim mechanic, was attacked by a mob during the massacre and eight years later cross-examined in the courtroom by the lawyers of the Hindu accused, whom he identified before the judge. Gafar was one of several survivors supported by Justice First (JF), a legal aid NGO helping Muslims to testify against Hindus. During the trial, the fact that he had survived the pogrom was used against him. The judge dismissed his testimony, noting that "there is mention [*sic*] of a mob of 3–4000 people stoning each other and that this stoning continued for half an hour and the witness [Gafar] fled to the mill to save his life at this time, therefore it is not possible to maintain that the witness could at that time recognize and identify the accused."[73] These comments illustrate the role of the law in creating a minority subject whose very existence (within the majority) precludes them from witnessing.

To compose the legal in the aftermath of violence means understanding how everyday law gives meaning to the categories of the minority and majority. To understand this process of how violence creates new subjects and subjectivity involves a shift away from the focus on exposing "the state" and more attention on the legal infrastructure—police writing, courtroom performances, temporalities of delay and deferral—that outlive the event. I use the word infrastructure here to reverse what is usually kept in the background of the legal process—as affect, procedure, and temporality—as neutral and passive. The legal here is constitutive of the conditions of possibility for not only killing minorities but an entire setup that frames, absorbs, and repackages political violence. In other words, what is often understood as legal violence, or the law's tendency to reenact trauma[74] and erase testimony, is better understood as the legal composition of minority subjects and subjectivities. In this sense, minorities within liberal states may *not* be formally stripped of rights[75] but are continually dismissed in the courtroom. They are subjects—who can be asked by judges to reconcile with neighbors who have stabbed and looted them, who can be told that they must choose between living and witnessing, and who are accused of being sectarian and malicious witnesses out to defame the majority.

Therefore, the idea that the law and the state collapsed in Gujarat[76] does not really square with the experience of Muslims who entered the courtroom to testify against their Hindu neighbors. It does not account for the courtroom as the space where Muslims were displaced from the place of witnessing and the experience of humiliation and powerlessness that Muslims faced *during* the trial. Seen through this lens, impunity is not some grand breakdown of the law or even a weakness of the state but the contribution of the law in the wider project of the minoritization of Muslims. The process was banal; the effects were remarkable. Muslim witnesses grew tired of wasting their days in lower courts: waiting for their case to be heard, waiting for the material evidence to be transferred to the appropriate court, waiting for the court administration to assign a judge to the case, waiting for the accused to stop skipping hearings, waiting for a judge to pronounce a judgment. They stopped coming to the court, suspected activists of colluding with the accused, "compromised" with the perpetrators, and ultimately refused to identify the accused in the courtroom.

Delay and deferral are key forms of temporality that allow political violence to be absorbed by ordinary courts. This is why political regimes in democracies are often able to use existing legal infrastructures to cleanse themselves of overwhelming complicity in political violence without resorting to special mechanisms of transitional justice.[77] This is different from the law's ability to erase and silence the victim's experience.[78] Instead of focusing on what the law knows or does not know, or even cannot know,[79] I show the painstaking legal accounting of violence that is also the condition of possibility for producing majority and minority subjects. If we approach the making of majorities and minorities as not simply an outcome of elections or a statistical exercise but one that is constantly produced through the making of "the legal" in the aftermath of political violence, then what emerges are legal practices that are inseparable from a wider political struggle to define the terms of citizenship within liberal-democratic regimes.

Such practices are not transgressions but are part of what Coutin and Yngvesson call "normal law"[80] and outlive political regimes and acts of mass murder. By studying this infrastructural aspect of the law, I address everyday law's relation to spectacular violence without "the stultifying assumption that states always uphold the law."[81]

In other words, what is often named as impunity and set aside from the everyday functioning of law within democracies as breakdown, a state of exception, corruption, and illegality, is also the construction of a legality.[82] Many Muslim survivors of the 2002 pogrom had survived previous events of mass violence—1969, 1985, 1992. Sometimes in the middle of a conversation, they would excavate yellowing legal papers wrapped in plastic bags from dusty trunks and suitcases to show me that they have proof. Proof of what? Proof that the law was not blind, incapable, or speechless. Proof that they had in the past too gone to the police station to file complaints about their shops burned, their missing and dead relatives, and their houses looted. Proof that they lived in a world divided into killable minorities and triumphant majorities.

Composing the Political

Consider the fact that Hindu mobs in Gujarat could have attacked Muslims under the cover of darkness but did not. They raped, murdered, maimed, burned, and looted in broad daylight for everyone to see. Similarly, in 1984, politicians and people in Delhi attacked Sikhs in full view of police and the wider public. In Colombo, again in 1984, Tamil neighborhoods were burned by their neighbors in full view of the police and the army. In light of such brazen punishment of minorities, it would be quite straightforward to make a case that this violence is emblematic of postcolonial states and their love of ghastly rituals. We could read state-sanctioned punishment of Muslims as sovereign violence: a premodern remnant of a politics where spectacular public punishment *still* exemplifies sovereign power. Such a reading would be strengthened by finding all the ways in which contemporary political regimes suspend the law and in effect work within a state of exception.[83] But if along with Foucault we consider performances of punishment as not merely negative acts but as technologies with specific relationships to the body, body politic, and techniques of violence, then we arrive at a different question: How does the pogrom compose the political?[84] Since the performance of sovereignty is always in dialogue with an audience,[85] and thus better understood as "a tentative and always emergent form of authority,"[86] then a reading of the form of violence can clarify our understanding of the form of the political produced during violence against minorities.

Put differently, what do we do with the fact that the attacks on Muslims did not merely inspire fear and suspend the rule of law but also created a distinct atmosphere? An atmosphere in which a large section of people—not all of whom were state actors or in positions of authority—came out onto the streets to kill and burn and loot? Not a passive state spectacle like a parade or a march when citizens are expected to see and cheer but a time to join and rejoice in the enactment of a mix of protest, murder, arson, and triumph. A time for ordinary Hindus to enjoy extraordinary power. A time when policemen looked away and even helped mobs as they as they broke into shops and looted them and set fire to mosques. A time when the police commissioner in a television interview to *Star News* on February 28, 2002, said, "These people [policemen], also, they somehow get carried away by the general sentiment. That's the whole trouble. The police are equally influenced by general sentiments." How do we analyze *this* arrangement of bodies, affects, time, and space? How do we account for the festive air that characterized the pogrom with some onlookers even telling an anthropologist that "they do this once a year"?[87] Lest one thinks all this is unique to India, one only needs to consider the long arc of antiminority pogroms in America,[88] Europe,[89] and South Asia.[90]

The structures of feeling that embed pogroms, therefore, cannot be circumscribed within the conventional analytics of state power.[91] For instance, the main protagonists of the attack in 2002, members of far-right Hindu groups like the *Bajrang Dal* and VHP, act like civil society groups but have strong relationships with the state and belong to the same "family" of Hindu nationalist organizations that include a right-wing political party like the BJP. This introduces a peculiar problem faced by analysts of pogroms and riots. After every incident of large-scale public antiminority violence, the analyst is asked to choose between the idea of a spontaneous riot *or* state-sanctioned genocide. Either to accept the colonial logic of timeless enmity between religious groups *or* yet again unmask the partisan state. One way out of this impasse, as Nugent and Krupa suggest, is to "off-center the state . . . to denaturalize it as the transcendental core of political life and the master symbol of political practice."[92] To focus on the form of violence helps us to "off-center" the state because pogroms bring together state and nonstate actors. Pogroms produce a popular will and endow "fictive" categories like the state and the people a unity and a personality.

To tackle this conviviality between state and nonstate actors that undergirds much of postcolonial violence,[93] we must abandon state-obsessed languages of complicity, sovereignty, and ideology, and look at the affective and performative work done by vernacular political forms.[94] The call for a *bandh* (shutdown)—the act of calling for a shutdown of the city—is not simply a reflection of state complicity but is better understood as a claim to make forms of rule legitimate. As a political technology, the Hindu nationalist call for a shutdown, affirmed by the ruling regime, invited Hindus across caste, class, and sectarian divisions to participate, witness, and relish the public punishment of Muslims. While the politics of exposure focuses on the role of Hindu nationalists and the police in facilitating the massacre, what is left out in such an analysis "are the practices through which bonds of identification and consent are solicited and bestowed (or not) on the agents of the state."[95] Put differently, antiminority violence is a key technique in postcolonial democracies to cohere (or *attempt* to cohere) claims to rule through invocations of Hindu, Sinhala, Islamic rule. If the "state effect" is to create a distinction between ostensibly autonomous entities like "the state" and "society," political violence against minorities play a decisive role in creating entities like "the people." In this way, the mass and public nature of the pogrom composes the violence on the street as an expression of popular sovereignty, and through the overt and covert participation of state actors in the violence, this "majority will" aligns itself with the state.

Let us return to the *bandh*. Because it was public, it was educational. There was no need to cover up the egregious atrocities against Muslims precisely because the *bandh* was not a simple instrument of state power, but an invitation to the public. It pushed large sections of the public indoors even as it created the conditions for many others to step out into the street as participants, spectators, looters, and arsonists. Terror for Muslims and a carnival for Hindus. The fact that actors across the political spectrum in South Asia use this political technique to empty streets, close markets, publicize grievances, and pressure ruling governments tells us that this is also a political technology that can compose new forms of the political.

As a form of performative crowd politics—collective looting, burning, stone throwing, and sloganeering—the *bandh* is not merely a curious detail of something we can then classify as state violence or ethnic conflict or even genocide. It is precisely the *bandh* form of public violence against minorities in postcolonial democracies that makes it inseparable from the normal democratic politics of protest and outrage.[96] As specific arrangements of bodies, temporalities, affects, and spaces, postcolonial pogroms are not, to repeat, merely a tool of the state, but moments in the formation of "the state" itself. To be clear, the *bandh*'s ability to hail people, produce bodies on the street, halt traffic, and shut down shops is not always a massacre or in support of the ruling government. In fact, political activists most often use it to *challenge* the ruling regime. But as a political technology, it always has the potential to become an expression of popular will, a wager for hegemony[97] that expands, reframes, and congeals *feelings* of what it means to be "the people."

What is truly political about postcolonial pogroms, then, is the power of forms of violence like the *bandh* to transform antiminority violence into popular sovereignty. It is the compositional work of the *bandh* to articulate antiminority violence with expressions of popular sovereignty that allows spectacular violence to forge majorities and minorities. This is a brief example of how this book moves from exposure to composition. Instead of exposing the complicity of the postcolonial state in killing minorities, I have explored a "minor" detail—the first seventy-two hours of the massacre. The arrangement of bodies, affects, and space during the pogrom did not end with the pogrom.

The first one and a half minutes of Rakesh Sharma's documentary film Final Solution *is grainy, noisy, and lit only by streetlights that are bright orange flares in the background. The camera is by the side of the street watching a convoy of trucks and motorbikes led by a stream of joyous men on foot. Firecrackers are popping, drums are beating, slogans are being shouted, and motorbikes and cars in the convoy are honking at the crowds gathered on the sides of the road with flags and garlands. Everywhere men in orange scarves and bandanas fill the frame. Writing in white appears at the bottom of the screen. "December 15, 2002. Right-wing* BJP-VHP *cadres celebrate Gujarat election victory." We are watching the victory procession of the Hindu nationalist party,* BJP, *after it won the elections in the aftermath of the pogrom. The camera cuts to a close-up shot of the face of a young man, a teenager in an orange bandana. "*BJP*'s victory is like our own. We have nothing more to say . . ." We see several boys in the background attracted to the camera like moths to the light. The camera rests on a boy's face, but suddenly a voice erupts out of the frame, and the camera jerks sharply to the right to show the face of another young boy with a soft face and glistening black eyes. He is singing an abusive rhyme against Muslims. His broad mischievous smile shows how much fun he is having on the street. We hear the filmmaker's voice asking the boy the meaning of the rhyme. The boy keeps repeating the rhyme until a third boy jumps into the frame, his hands cupped to his mouth to make sure the camera can hear him shout sexual expletives about Muslims above the din of the firecrackers, drumbeat, and the traffic.*[98]

Rethinking Democracy

If we understand democracy less as a fixed regime type, a checklist (free and fair elections, rule of law, etc.), but rather as a specific configuration of the majority-minority relationship in law, public culture, and politics, then a compositional reading of political violence can create an opening to rethink the relationship between violence, the rule of law, the making of minorities, and the performance of democracy. But some may object that isn't democracy fundamentally about ideas of plurality, multiplicity, and difference? Isn't it perverse, then, to suggest that antiminority violence is not an anomaly but constitutive of democracy?

Democracy institutes a relationship between number and rule that locks societies in a path that can seem like there are only two binary choices: either minority or majority rule. In his examination of the inscription of democracy in postcolonial states, David Scott argues that the introduction of democracy is a "a whole new game of politics" based on abstract number as an integral aspect of democratic rationality. And that discussions are often limited to safeguards to protect minorities that do not undo the majority-minority relationship itself.[99] This limitation within democratic theory and practice is critical because we know that formal minority rights and constitutional safeguards have not protected minorities from public violence. The category of the minority itself seems double-edged in so far as liberal theory's impulse to enshrine the minority in law and culture (to protect it from the dominance of the majority) is always in tension with the abstract idea of the citizen within a modern state. In this sense, the secular idea of the abstract citizen is also in tension with Christian history of the minority as a group that is unequal to the majority and thus requires special protection from it.[100]

Keeping in mind the ongoing minoritization of groups within a democracy and the limits of liberal discussions on how to safeguard minorities (since these discussions do not seek to undo the majority-minority bind), we have to abandon the space carved out for antiminority violence within normative political theory—as aberration, interruption, and exception.[101] We have to guard against the tendency to think of pogroms as cases of disorder, a pathology of South Asian culture and politics, and the breakdown of the rule of law. And despite the active involvement of "the state," political violence against minorities does not begin and end at its doorstep. This does not mean a disregard for the postcolonial state's repeated use of violence against minorities in South Asia to win elections:[102] pogroms against Tamils in Colombo, against Sikhs in Delhi, and most recently against Rohingyas in Myanmar. However, by paying attention to the patterning of this violence, its distribution across state and nonstate domains, and its absorption within everyday law, popular politics, mainstream media, and human rights activism, this book shows that pogroms and their afterlives produce majorities and minorities within a democracy.[103]

Public violence against minorities (often labeled as communal riots in South Asia) can help us to rethink democracy in two ways: In the conventional sense, pogroms strengthen the power of states to govern a divided and unequal society, polarize a fractured electorate, and create an "us" versus "them." In other words, "the people" as an identifiable and governable category within democracies is often created in the shadow of public violence against minorities. But antiminority violence is also embedded within democracies in a more *infrastructural* sense—not a pathology of culture but as part of the procedures that comprise "due process" itself.[104] Democracies contain within them a binary machine—embedded in electoral mobilization, police writing, legal trials, and media—that polarizes a society into historically shifting formations of violent majorities and vulnerable minorities.

When violence against minorities is spectacular, public, and festive, and forge new forms of belonging and intimacy, existing varieties of democratic theory are not helpful. This is primarily because these theories depend on concepts of repression and erasure that assume that violence destroys and corrupts democracy. They also begin with the widely held assumption at the heart of modern theories of state formation[105] that political subjection and state power must be masked to be effective.[106] In this book, in contrast, violence against minorities and the way it is transformed by law, media, and politics help us to analyze the forces that are pushing democracies across the world to become societies of enmity,[107] an enmity that is no longer masked by the veneer of rights and laws. By looking at crowd politics, courtroom procedures, police writing, legal temporalities, and public affects that transform public violence against minorities into popular democratic rule, I want to bring postcolonial violence into the heart of democracy's relationship with violence. To put it in the form of a question, if we accept that violence is constitutive of the modern nation-state, then how do democracies capture, absorb, and reproduce wounded majorities and killable minorities?

This is not just another way of repeating Tocqueville's premonition that democracy can always turn into the tyranny of the majority.[108] The kinds of majority/minority discussed here is not a stable representational bloc, or statistical entity, as much as an affective entity, a waxing and waning that courses through the veins of modern democracies. It is built up of moods and performances, inscribed in official archives and mainstream newspapers and forms of affect—an improbable mix of persecution and glory—that allow members of a particular group to enact and experience fantasies of power and community. In other words, democracies by periodically conceding the power of life and death to racial, religious, and ethnic suprema-cist groups does not suffer a lack of legitimacy if such forms of targeted death and destruction are also linked to what Lauren Berlant calls a "na-tional fantasy"[109]—Hindu nation in India is in this sense not a breakdown of democracy but a moment to understand democracy's radical transforma-tion through antiminority politics. This national fantasy is not a perversion of the modern nation-state but is essential to the disjuncture between the state as the guarantor of rights and the nation as the fantasy of a homog-enous people. If we consider a different context, for instance, in the case of the killing of Black people by the police in the United States, the minority is yet again produced through public violence, and significant differences in the performance of violence (men in uniform killing unarmed civilians in the case of the United States) should not distract us from the larger point about the space of racial and ethnic supremacy in liberal democracies.

The capacity of antiminority violence to strengthen the ability of mod-ern democracies to rule gives a twist to the idea that liberal democracy cov-ets crowds but fears riots.[110] At certain historical conjunctures, democracies covet riots and pogroms precisely because they cohere diverse and contra-dictory interests under a single umbrella. Even if this coherence is fictive and ephemeral, it is one way to fill the "hollow at the centre of the idea of democ-racy itself."[111] It is well known that democracy, unlike other types of regimes, does not really have a fundamental principle (except the expansion of liberty) at its core. Since democracy cannot be regulated by concepts of excellence or blood or order, or for that matter coercion, it needs an outside animat-ing force to bind "the people" with "the state." Public violence against mi-norities becomes one of many ways to fill the "empty space" at the heart of democracies.[112]

This empty space is of course never empty for too long, and political violence is a moment of opening, a window of opportunity, when state and nonstate actors seize the power of the crowd, documentary and media regimes, and law to fill this empty space, to (re)define the relationship between "the state" and "the people" and a crucial third term, "the majority." In this con-text, postcolonial democracies reveal the compatibility of public violence against minorities with the everyday work of liberal democracy—the con-ducting of free and fair elections, the writing of police reports, the gathering and presentation of legal evidence, and the performance of trials. Within democracies, the concept of popular sovereignty, the people, is always being split into a majority and minority. Of course, this splitting is not necessarily violent or even undesirable. This splitting is in fact integral to the functioning of politics itself when such majorities and minorities are the outcome of political processes.[113] But what happens when a political majority seeks to transform itself into a permanent majority?

Postcolonial democracies like India are good to think with precisely because we are not able to shield theories of democracy behind the veil of exceptionalism, and keep democracy and its other—fascism, authoritarianism, and totalitarianism—in two separate worlds. The question is not whether democracies are more or less violent than authoritarian regimes, but what can India tell us about the power of public violence against minorities to act as a catalyst for the creation of a permanent majority? Given the widely held consensus (which is crumbling in the light of Trump's America and the post-Brexit United Kingdom) that Western liberal democracy should be the ideal that democracies in other parts of the world must strive for, it is important to distinguish the endeavor of this book from Western philosophy's enduring suspicion of democracy. From Plato to Madison, democracy has long been associated with chaos that typically topples into tyranny. If democracy is about extending the power to rule others to the many (not the one or few), then the fear of mob violence is always looming on the horizon of liberal political theory.[114] This book is not a lament about the threat of anarchy that looms over the messy concept of democracy but a recognition that violence against minorities energizes and animates our democracies and the task of rethinking democracy cannot sidestep this problem.

Overview

If the introduction was a passage that led the reader through the core problem of the book—the limits of exposing violence, and what is at stake in taking the risk of writing and reading beyond exposure—then I imagine each chapter of the book as a path that radiates outwards and can be taken in any order depending on the reader's interest. In each chapter, I take objects I encountered while doing fieldwork in the aftermath of the Gujarat pogrom—the event, the archive, the witness, the trial, anti-impunity activism, the fact-finding report, and the newspaper article—and suggest a compositional approach to work with them.

Chapter 1, "A Minor Reading," opens with an archetypical scene of a riot in Ahmedabad in 2011. A tale of arson and stoning between Hindus and Muslims that circulates in English and Gujarati newspapers as yet another instance of primitive violence between antagonistic communities in a "riot-prone" neighborhood. The plot is basic and familiar: a minor argument between a Hindu and Muslim erupts into full-fledged rioting. Rather than trying to expose the patent falsity of this colonial master narrative of Hindus and Muslims perpetually at war with each other, I follow the minor as "what everyone knows." What everyone knows in this case is the fact that Muslims in the neighborhood describe the so-called riot as an organized attack on their shops by a well-known local criminal. What seems at first brush gossip about petty criminal characters helps me to interrupt how public information about anti-Muslim violence circulates. A minor reading offers a composition of violence that is articulated by minorities for minorities within intimate settings. Such a reading begins by focusing on that which ostensibly requires no explanation: the trigger incident that is both on the surface and left unexplained within the narratives of the riot. A minor reading is not the exposure of a hidden truth but more akin to pulling at a slight thread on the surface of the scene of violence until it connects mainstream media and everyday law into a machine that frames conflict in terms of *religious* difference. But a minor reading is also a reminder of what escapes this binary making machine: efforts by Muslims to imagine a world beyond Hindus versus Muslims.

In chapter 2, "Composing the Archive," I read police First Information Reports (FIRs) made during the violence in 2002 through minor forms that lie on the surface of the police archive—such as aggregation, repetition, and the trace. These minor forms connect the exceptional with the routine and the colonial to the postcolonial. The chapter asks whether exposure is the only way to read archives of violence and shows that the most explicit features of police reporting comprise the archival infrastructure of anti-Muslim violence. By offering a compositional response to the problem of working with what Derrida called an "archive of the destruction of the archive,"[115] the chapter tracks the forms of time and space that connect archives with technologies of antiminority violence like the *bandh* (shutdown). By making the case that archives of violence do not simply erase but also repeat, temporalize, and aggregate, I draw attention to forms within archives that exceed the event and ideology. This world-making capacity of the archive of violence to constitute killable minorities does not derive solely from the law; it shares, incorporates, attests, and embeds narratives and affects that circulate in the media and Hindu nationalist speeches.

In chapter 3, "Against the Witness," I analyze trials in the lower courts of Ahmedabad that do not simply silence the witness but also displace them from the space of witnessing itself. Turning to the failure of testimony in the courtroom, I compose scenes that could be read as scenes of legal erasure into scenes of minoritization. I argue that the inability of Muslim witnesses to testify in the courtroom against their Hindu neighbors is part of a wider process of *becoming* a minority. What has been described famously as the "crisis of witnessing" in literary studies and philosophy—the limits of law to represent violence beyond language—is reframed in this chapter as a process of producing a minority that can see but not witness their property looted, their homes burned, and their families raped and tortured. This process builds on the chasm between individual testimony and collective violence and seizes the legal infrastructure—police documents, cross-examination techniques, and legal reasoning—to produce Muslims as false witnesses. Minorities who are then refuted by police documents, their own previous statements to the police, the scale and nature of the attacks on them, and finally even by the very fact of their survival.

Chapter 4, "Anti-Impunity Activism," examines the limits of anti-impunity activism that conceptualizes impunity as a force external to the law. I follow the work of JF, a legal aid nongovernmental organization that helped Muslim survivors to testify against their Hindu neighbors in the courtroom as part of a larger struggle for justice and rights. Justice First understood the legal process as an effort to restore the constitutional rights of Muslims in India and a moral war to uphold liberal values such as secularism. After the painstaking task of persuading hundreds of Muslims to fight for justice, most of the cases crumbled in the courtroom, as survivors grew disenchanted with the legal process. Like anti-impunity politics elsewhere, JF's efforts focused on the punishment of individual perpetrators. But this effort to expose impunity was based on legal reasoning, rituals, and procedures that were inextricable from the socio-legal relationships that produced anti-Muslim violence. For instance, the key role of the police and state actors in facilitating the pogrom. By examining the challenges faced by the JF activists and lawyers as they tried to use the law to fight for justice, this chapter shows the double-edged quality of legal exposure: the attempt to expose Hindu perpetrators in the courtroom also exposed vulnerable and poor Muslims to legal violence including the documentary and temporal power of the state apparatus. Finally, as the binaries that guide anti-impunity efforts—rule of law versus impunity, speech versus forgetting, victims versus perpetrators—dissolved over time, anti-impunity politics was unable to account for ethical frameworks that Muslim survivors were using to reconstruct their life based on neighborliness, secrecy, and cooperation.

Chapter 5, "Beyond the Unspeakable," turns to sexual violence, which is often conceptualized as unspeakable and beyond representation. And yet, activists and scholars produce valuable and rich accounts of the widespread circulation and weaponization of sexual violence as an essential aspect of political violence against minorities. How could sexual violence both persist in testimony, human rights activism, scholarly accounts, media reports, and the courtroom and yet be invisible and unspeakable? This paradox leads to the key problem at the heart of the chapter: How do we compose sexual violence in conditions of simultaneous visibility and erasure? I respond by tracking the scene of sexual violence as it moves through human rights reports, activist encounters, police documents, and ends up in the courtroom as exaggeration. By paying attention to the different ways in which sexual violence appears, circulates, and persists inside and outside the courtroom, I compose the object sexual violence not as an isolated act, an unspeakable action, or a traumatic memory, but words and actions that constitute the scene of violence and its afterlife in the police station, courtroom, and activist practice. By recomposing sexual violence against Muslim women as constitutive of the pogrom, not merely as an isolated event but as a practice and language that persists in the police station, courtroom, and the parliament, we can get a better sense of how Muslim women—and their bodies—are attacked not simply on the street but when they appear before the law. As an inspiration to compose the force of sexual violence outside a singular event, I turn to an eight-channel video installation by the artist Amar Kanwar that moves us from the forensic to the poetic.

A Minor Reading

ON THE MORNING OF MAY 2, 2011, I opened Gujarat's best-selling daily[1] *Gujarat Samachar* (Gujarat News) and saw the headline "Violence [*toofan*] in the area between Idgah Circle and Asarwa Bridge: 15 vehicles—shops burned." A *toofan* (literally storm) referred here to violence between Hindus and Muslims in Madhavpura. As chance would have it, I had been visiting this "riot-prone" neighborhood for over a year to meet with Muslim survivors and witnesses working with Justice First (JF). When people described Madhavpura as riot-prone they meant that along with neighborhoods like Kalupur and Dariyapur, some neighborhoods in Eastern Ahmedabad frequently witnessed violence between Hindus and Muslims. In these neighborhoods, residents and the police often brace themselves for periodic "rioting." Many people I spoke to even had a sense of the "where" (Eastern part of the city) and "when" (religious festivals) one could expect the eruption of the next *toofan* (storm) or *dhamaal*.[2] Madhavpura was a major flashpoint in 2002 as well. During my visits, I chatted with Muslim witnesses while Bharatbhai, a paralegal, checked their legal papers, updated them on the status of their case, and, if the trial had begun, helped them rehearse the statements they were going to make in court.

Nestled next to a major arterial road, this neighborhood had a substantial number of Hindus and Muslims living next to each other. Surrounded by now abandoned textile mills,[3] the neighborhood comprised mainly poor Muslims and Hindus who were self-employed or engaged in manual labor.

Muslims lived in small pockets, encircled by largely Hindu colonies. In 2002, Muslim residents had gathered in one colony to defend themselves from large Hindu mobs and were largely successful in minimizing the loss of life but could not save their shops and businesses.

The JF office was abuzz with the news of the latest *dhamaal* in Ahmedabad. Bharatbhai, a JF paralegal who was responsible for cases in Madhavpura, was worried about his witnesses. Madhavpura was only fifteen minutes away from the JF office, and we decided to make a quick visit. After covering our faces, arms, and necks from the blazing sun outside (it was over 45 degrees Celsius), we biked through the narrow and winding streets of the old city to finally stop in front of a shop. The shop was at the intersection of two busy streets that merged to form a traffic intersection called the "Idgah circle"—the site where Hindu and Muslim mobs had allegedly attacked each other last night. A mosque, which was destroyed by Hindu mobs in 2002, had been rebuilt and stood like a lighthouse at the intersection.

We stopped at Jafar's shop, an elderly Muslim man who owned a bottled water business. Whenever Bharat and I passed Jafar's shop, Bharat would slow down his motorcycle before the shop and exchange greetings with him over the traffic. They had known each other since 2006, when Bharat enlisted Jafar as a community-based volunteer of JF. Such volunteers were not paid by JF but were the "locals" who had helped JF begin work in new and unfamiliar neighborhoods when it first started out and wanted to recruit as many Muslim witnesses as possible for its movement for justice. Jafar was also a member of the Madhavpura "peace committee," a reminder of the official recognition of the neighborhood's propensity for communal violence. The peace committee comprised a group of six Hindus and six Muslims appointed by the police to maintain peace in the area.

Outside Jafar's shop, I noticed signs of "rioting." These were the scenes of arson that had accompanied the newspaper report: photographs of burnt cars and bicycles, stones, shards of glass on the street, a makeshift police post, and broken shop fronts. Drugged by the blazing sun, two policemen were sleeping inside a police jeep parked right outside the shop. We entered the shop, exchanged greetings with Jafar, and asked him about the charred piece of metal outside the shop. It was his new car. Jafar's shop was more like a garage since it had no doors, only an iron shutter that faced a busy street. In the day, Jafar and his employees sat inside the shop, amid electric water coolers and empty four-foot-high plastic containers of purified water that are used in offices and homes.

In the last two days, Jafar had lost a motorbike, a car, and lots of water bottles. As we chatted with him, business went on as usual in the shop. His sons loaded vehicles with fresh water bottles, and a steady stream of customers asked for pocket-sized refrigerated plastic bags of water called "pouches." We were handed a pouch each to sip while he told us what happened. "It happened during the night and no one was around. No one saw anything." Everyone in the shop kept quiet. I was confused. Here was a man who had suffered a huge loss but was eager not to blame anyone. "After all no one was around in the night, so what can be done?" Jafar said more than once. But then a worker who was loading water bottles spoke up.

"*Everyone knows* it's Dhoni's work, the local hoodlum [*goonda*] in the area."

Dhoni—the name struck a chord. I had heard stories about his role in the violence in 2002 from paralegals and remembered reading his name in a police report. During previous trips to this neighborhood, Bharat had pointed out a row of shops not far away from Jafar's shop that gave Dhoni "protection" (*hafta*) money. The comment sparked a conversation that Jafar reluctantly later joined:

MAN 1: Even the police are afraid of him [Dhoni]. He extorts money from the entire row of shops near the end of the road. That shop, the one that sells tires is on a street where many shops pay him protection money. He pays the cops off with money because he is a bootlegger[4] so he makes good money selling liquor. He is an accused in the 2002 violence as well.

JAFAR: I am a part of the peace committee here. There are twelve members in the peace committee, six Hindus and six Muslims, and *everyone knows him*, but the Hindus never give his name to the police. He and his boys came from the Hindu side and burned down some of the shops in this area, including my car. I did give his name and that's why the police stationed a SRP [Special Reserve Police] check post at the circle.

MAN 2: Even they [pointing to the half-asleep policemen outside] are afraid of him. *Everyone knows that.* Once he chased the local BJP councilor [politician] down the main road brandishing a sword! His liquor business allows him to pay off the police and even senior police inspectors fear him in this area . . .

I was struck by the cascading effect of a stray comment about "what everyone knew." Immediately after the comment, people began exchanging stories about Dhoni. It was something, all the men repeated, "that everyone knows." Everyone except me. As I listened to the exchange between the people in the shop, I wondered how to square what I was hearing in the shop with what I had read in the newspaper. Here was a tale anchored to a single protagonist, with links to the police, and on the other hand there was the impersonal eruption of religious violence that was reported in the newspaper. Let us read the main part of the newspaper report:

> Elements that were successful in breaking communal (*quami*) harmony in the Madhavpura communal build-up on Saturday acted again on Sunday.... In the evening violent [*toofani*] mobs burned around 15 vehicles and shops in the area between Idgah circle and Asarwa Bridge. Within an hour of the incident on Saturday night between two youths over the exchange of money, two units of the Rapid Action Force and police have been deployed in the area.
>
> On Saturday evening, near the Idgah circle at around 11:30 p.m., one man named Dinesh alias Dhoni Nadiya bought a CD from a youth named Allahbraksha, who sells CDs and DVDs there. An argument ensued between them when Dinesh refused to pay. Allahbraksha beat Dinesh for being rowdy and not paying for the CDs. Mobs of both communities confronted each other as soon as people heard about this incident. Between 11 p.m. to 12 a.m., the mobs of both communities pelted stones and damaged shops and carts. Since there were a large number of people from both communities in the mobs, all the police force available was called in.... In about an hour after the riot [*dhamaal*], the situation was brought under control... 15–20 rioters [*toofanio*] were detained. At 10 in the night, when this was written, an uneasy peace prevailed in the area amidst strict police presence.

Note the difference between "what everyone knows" and "elements successful in breaking communal harmony." From the newspaper report, you would never guess that Dhoni is no ordinary man. There is nothing in it about his notoriety and his past. Unlike the conversation in Jafar's shop, the newspaper report describes a conflict between two communities, unnamed yet named, marked by their antagonism for each other, and unmarked insofar as they are purely affective entities—mobs. Unlike what people in Jafar's shop were telling each other—something that "everyone knew" but still needed to be told and affirmed publicly through each other, the newspaper report simply mentions the identifiably Hindu and Muslim names Dhoni and Allahbraksha as a sign for something beyond the two men and the event.

Put differently, the newspaper report describes the disturbance of everyday life by religious violence; the men in Jafar's shop describe criminal violence as part of everyday life.

What do we do with these two very different narratives of violence that also point to two very different forms of violence? What seems at first brush to be mere gossip about a bootlegger in the aftermath of a riot is a form of speech, for minorities like Muslims in Ahmedabad, to interrupt the ways in which information about Hindus, Muslims, and violence circulates in the public sphere. It is perhaps even a counternarrative to the official discourse about Hindus and Muslims in Madhavpura. I call what I heard in Jafar's shop that day a "minor reading." By minor reading, I have in mind a reading that composes the scene of violence to emphasize the agency of minor characters and how information circulates in minor spaces (e.g., the shop or the community newspaper) to interrupt the forms of address that constitute the relationship and conception of the majority and the minority as permanent entities.

A minor reading of "Hindu-Muslim" riots, or what is often called ethnic violence, allows us to understand how mainstream media frame antiminority violence as well as the forms of narrative that challenge it. To be clear, my aim is not to unmask "what really happened" but rather to attend to "what everyone knows." I track the way violence attaches itself to a neighborhood, examine the forms that normalize its enactment and genres that circulate it as public information, and finally describe the efforts, successful or not, of minor spaces to interrupt the official and mainstream media publics around anti-Muslim violence.

But why analyze a small, localized incident that takes place several years after the state-wide public attacks against Muslims in 2002? Because there are structural similarities between the two events. The disjuncture between "what everyone knows" and what circulates as public discourse about communal riots is not restricted to one locality and one incident in India. The same disjuncture also characterized the attacks on Muslims in 2002. Even as human rights activists described the violence in 2002 as a genocide or pogrom, the government and mainstream media called it a "riot." This disjuncture is not limited to reports about violence, but it is especially stark in violence against minorities in India.

Public, state-sanctioned violence against minorities poses a definitional problem right at the beginning: What word should we use to describe a largely one-sided public attack on religious minorities that is supported by the government, the police, and the wider public? Most Gujaratis, including vernacular newspapers, use terms like *dhamaal* (chaos) and *toofaan* (storm) that do not correspond to either the activist's genocide or the state's riot. Human rights activists, NGOs, and civil society challenge the characterization of targeted violence as communal riots because it suggests that the violence is spontaneous, impacts Hindus and Muslims equally, and is motivated by religious differences. The label riot masks the role of actors and institutions like Hindu nationalist groups, state officials, local politicians, and the police in the attacks against Muslims. This struggle around the naming of antiminority violence and activist efforts to expose its true name is also a larger struggle to make and unmake publics around the scene of violence.

This struggle is not only about meaning and definition but also about constituting a public. As Michael Warner argues, "when people address publics, they engage in struggles . . . over the conditions that bring them together as a public."[5] This struggle cannot be reduced to the official versus the unofficial, the state versus the subaltern, but is about the role of specific forms of publicity around violence—a mixture of text, genre, plot, and affect—that delineate the majority/minority relationship. In other words, the struggle to find the correct name for a form of antiminority violence that is neither state nor nonstate is inseparable from the wider struggle faced by minority groups to articulate and participate in a public sphere that defines what it means to be a Hindu and a Muslim. Does this make anti-Muslim violence a public secret?[6] Not really. After all, for whom is the violence in Madhavpura a secret? To be clear, all public discourse minoritizes some bodies and experiences since it is built on the fiction of universality and self-effacement.[7] So what is at stake here is not simply that the mainstream media and official narratives mischaracterize anti-Muslim violence as religious riots, but how a minor reading attempts to challenge the idea that majorities and minorities are fixed entities.

Scholars have analyzed the disjuncture between what everyone knows and what circulates as official knowledge as part of the "epistemic murk" that surrounds violence. Michael Taussig uses the concept of the "public secret" to understand the difference between what is known and what is said and what people know not to know.[8] But what if groups that face recurrent and targeted violence are more than willing to speak about it, and are clear about the actors and structures that harm them, and yet their story does not produce a public, does not take off, fails to circulate beyond minor spaces? In such a context, the making and unmaking of publics around violence is part of the wider process of the making of majorities and minorities itself.

To show how this process works, I follow the circulation of talk, news, and police reports of the single event that opened this chapter. I describe the minor—as scale, trigger, detail, the personal, and form of discourse—that comprise the "Hindu-Muslim riot." The minor points to the importance of narrative in giving intelligibility to violence,[9] and its role as a radical mediation[10]—the arrangements that do not simply communicate but transform the entities they connect. By this I mean the power of mainstream media to insert actors, spaces, and events within narratives that produce the majority and the minority. What these media representations and official documents are however unable to account for is the minor, whether it is the "spark" that leads to the mobilization of crowds, the gaps in the neat temporality of the spontaneous riot, or the voices of those who speak of new kinds of majorities and minorities.

What Makes the Minor Minor?

The Gujarat government in its report to the National Human Rights Commission of India made a case that the attacks on Muslims in 2002 were unremarkable. Their argument was based on a particular arrangement of the major and minor in the "natural" history of communal violence in Gujarat:

> The State of Gujarat has a long history of communal riots. Major riots have been occurring periodically in the State since 1969. Two commissions of inquiry—Jagmohan Reddy Commission of Inquiry, 1969 and Dave Commission of Inquiry, 1985 were constituted to go into the widespread communal violence that *erupted from time to time* . . . between 1970 and 2002 Gujarat has witnessed 443 *major* communal riots. Even *minor* altercations, over *trivial* matters like kite flying have led to communal violence (emphasis mine).[11]

Irrespective of the scale, location, and actors in the 443 events that occurred from 1970 to 2002, this official response subsumes all these events under the category of the communal riot. By stressing the eruption of riots over "trivial matters," it normalizes public violence and inserts 2002 into a stable history of antagonism between Hindus and Muslims, a natural history of religious violence. The riot is the thread that weaves hundreds of events across three decades all across the state into a tapestry of unending war between Hindus and Muslims. What the Gujarat government wants to really say is this: If kite flying can lead to violence between Hindus and

Muslims, then what do you expect will happen when a Muslim mob burns a train and fifty-nine Hindus along with it?

While this long history of communal riots in Gujarat is often repeated in mainstream media and then critiqued in scholarly and activist work, I want to emphasize the role of the minor here. The so-called minor events that are the trigger for "eruptions" of violence between Hindus and Muslims seem to carry a weight that is hardly trivial. How do we move so quickly and effortlessly from the minor to the major? Numerous studies show us the complicity of state actors and the police in attacks on minorities, but I want us to pause and ask what makes the minor *minor*?

The differences between 2002 and 2011 are important: the violence in 2002 spread across nineteen districts of Gujarat and led to the deaths of more than two thousand Muslims, whereas the incident in Madhavpura did not lead to any deaths and was limited to one neighborhood in Ahmedabad. And yet it is precisely the minor key of the event in 2011 that can help us get a grip on the long-term, enduring, and everyday processes of news-making around violence that create Hindus and Muslims as antagonistic communities ready to go to war "over trivial matters."

In both cases, 2002 and 2011, Muslims contest the official narrative and provide competing narratives to explain the violence. It is only the ignoring of the minor that allows the history of a region (Gujarat) and a city (Ahmedabad) to become the history of violence between Hindus and Muslims. Some histories begin their analysis of riots in Gujarat as far back as the eighteenth century (1714). Media reportage, scholarly writing, and official reports often list this long history of "communal riots" in Ahmedabad: 1941, 1942, 1946, 1956, 1958, 1964, 1969, 1974, 1981, 1985–86, 1990, and 1992–93. Gyanendra Pandey argues that such a seamless history of violence and religious animosity is a mode of writing history that reifies colonial categories.[12] Deepak Mehta and Roma Chatterji point out that "it is through the act of narration that clusters of incidents acquire the status of a critical event. Official documents, investigative reports and oral testimonies are all narrative acts that contribute to the crystallization of the event of violence."[13] Thus, despite the different causes, spaces, and actors in scenes of violence, a range of narrative acts—state, media, and scholarly writing—give the riot a coherence and ubiquity across time and space.[14] This allows it to subsume competing narratives like the ones offered by people in Jafar's shop.

The coherence of the riot is based on multiple factors. First, it is based on the popularity of the concept of communalism as a cultural ideology that affects politics and society in India and South Asia more generally. Communalism as ideology and political practice allows "local" events to become yet another instance of "communalism" in South Asia.[15] Pandey defines communalism as "political movements and activities based on the proclaimed common interests (economic, cultural, political) of members of a religious community (or communities), in opposition to the politics and activities of members of another religious community, and to the real or imagined threat from these."[16]

Pandey argues that the communal riot was produced in the colonial archive in the nineteenth century. The "master narrative of the riot," broadly conceived, is a narrative of primordial and irrational hatred between antagonistic religious communities—Hindus versus Muslims. As a narrative *form*, it subsumes local details and actually replaces class and caste dynamics with an ethnic theory of violence. There are certain formulaic elements in the colonial narrative of the riot—trigger event, frenzied crowd, and the establishment of law and order—and it functions as a "master narrative." His analysis shows how colonial accounts of the riot keep changing, including the site of the conflict, the number of dead, and the causes for the conflict. This shows that the "bare facts of the situation were *constructed*—and constructed out of the prejudices, biases and 'common sense' of the writers."[17]

Despite the place and time of the riot—from Ahmedabad's earliest "riot" in the eighteenth century to Gujarat 2002—the riot has a formulaic sequence: it begins with a random, trivial event, what is often called a trigger or spark, which erupts into violence between two communities, most commonly Hindus and Muslims. The trigger event is fungible yet predictable; it can be anything from a festival to "kite flying." Take for instance the newspaper report that opens this chapter. A fight between a Hindu and a Muslim over the purchase of a CD that led to rioting in Madhavpura. Similarly, according to official accounts of the attack on Muslims in 2002, Muslims attacked a train that led to the death of fifty-nine Hindus in Godhra, and this sparked off arson, loot, rape, and murder across the state. At some point, the police arrive on the scene and dispel the mobs, and peace reigns again, until, of course, the next minor event sparks off rioting.

In other words, the communal riot is prefabricated colonial discourse congealed into a narrative that circulates in mainstream media and state institutions like law courts. From this, one can argue that the framing of violence against Muslims in postcolonial India as a "riot" is simply the power of the state to justify forms of politics based on seeing the population as

Hindus and Muslims, majorities and minorities, antagonistic to each other. What I want to emphasize here is that this *form* is not merely a sign of state power writ large. Even as it shows the enduring force of colonial categories, and its persistence into the postcolonial, this form of writing has tentacles far beyond the confines of "the state."

Police Composition

"Keep it, it's a copy, I have the original for insurance," Jafar said, handing me a copy of his police report as I left his shop. It was the First Information Report (FIR) describing the cognizable offense, the time and place of incident, the relevant offenses [as per the Indian Penal Code (IPC)], the names and addresses of the accused, and the details of the person who reported these crimes to the police. The author of the report was the Assistant Police Inspector (ASI) who worked from a police station in walking distance from the shop.

The police had classified the offenses under IPC sections 143 (unlawful assembly), 147 (rioting), 148 (armed rioting), 149, 135, 337, 427 (damaging public property), and Bombay Police Act 135 (2). Most of these provisions, especially IPC 143, 147, and 148 were also used during the violence in 2002. Let me quote the police report in detail (my translation):

> This is a complaint of yesterday's incident on 30.4.2011 at around 2330 when *Hindu-Muslim mobs* confronted each other, pelted stones and damaged property related to [*anusandhane*] an incident of fighting regarding the purchase of a cassette at the cassette shop near the Idgah circle...
>
> At around 7 p.m. members of the *Hindu community* came in a mob from the side of Jugaldas colony and members of the *Muslim community* came in a mob from the Pathan colony and confronted each other at the Idgah circle... pelting stones at each other and *mobs of both communities numbering around 500 each came* with weapons like pipes and sticks in their hands. While stoning each other they started burning shops and vehicles near the Idgah circle... finally mobs of both communities were dispersed.

The police report includes all the elements of the "master narrative" of the communal riot: a confrontation between Hindu and Muslim "communities" sparked off by a fight "over the purchase of a cassette." We see two religious *communities*—Hindus and Muslims—pelting stones at each other and damaging property. Like ancient wars when armies launched attacks from clearly marked areas at a mutually settled time, Hindus and Muslims seem to act in coordination. But the symmetry doesn't really tell us why. Why is all this happening?

Notice that the police incident connects "hundreds" of people stoning each other and burning shops and vehicles to another prior incident of fighting over a cassette. The brevity of the police report signals its adaptability; it is more fable, less description. The police inspector joins the two events—let us call them the minor and the major—with a simple noun "relate" (*anusandhane*, which means in connection with what has gone before). One thing after another—that's all it takes to join the two temporally separate events—the trigger and the riot, the minor and the major.

Much scholarship on riots in South Asia shows that the concept of the riot gives agency to mobs not individuals.[18] Individual agency and motivation are sidestepped to foreground community in this story. The key actors involved are not identified (but they are arrested later along with twenty-nine others), and no motivation is attributed to the unmarked incident around the cassette or how the event flared into something *more* than simply fighting between individuals. In the police report, the minor incident has no significance in itself: it is simply there to get you from point A to point B—to tie cause to effect.

The mise-en-scène of the police report skillfully uses space—composed of contiguous but segregated Hindu and Muslim neighborhoods—to paint a picture of a symmetrical war. The report organizes the space of violence in the mode of a war: naming the neighborhoods from where Hindu and Muslim mobs *originate* and where they clash. The "mobs" have no subjectivity (they are affectively charged entities that need no motivation) and are identified only by their religious identity, which explains the violence. This could very easily be a nineteenth-century colonial report.

Hindus emerge from a "Hindu colony," and Muslims emerge from a "Muslim colony" identified by unambiguous religious identifiers [*Jugaldas* colony versus *Pathan* colony] to confront each other at the crossroads (*Idgah* circle) that separates the two communities like a border.[19] It is remarkable how much symmetry is used to compose the chaos. On the surface of the report, there is a tension between the artificial symmetry of the police narrative and the idea of the riot as an eruption. Notice that both Hindu and Muslim mobs are "500 each," carry identical weapons, and emerge at the same time (7 p.m.).

As the narrative of the police report progresses, space and religion become indistinguishable; religious identity is mapped onto specific residential colonies, which in turn blur into spaces of origin for violent mobs. In other words, the FIR as a composition brings together heterogeneous elements (spaces, actors, and affect) to stabilize the event as religious violence. Inside the report, space trumps action, affect trumps character, and religious identity is the glue that holds everything together. In sum, the appearance of collective violence (major event) after an altercation over the purchase of a cassette (minor event) hinges on the subordination of the minor to the major. The minor must remain a mere spark for something more important to come. As we read beyond the police report, I will show that what makes police writing so powerful is not only its status within law as proof, or even its connection to colonial technologies of governance, but rather its power to strike the first blow to the minor.

Circulation

With these elements of the police report in mind, let us see how the riot travels beyond the law. This is how the Gujarati newspaper *Sandesh* (literal meaning: Message) described the events in Madhavpura. Here are two reports:

> Mobs of both communities clashed with each other yesterday late in the night near Idgah circle, Madhavpura. An altercation between two youths last night took a deadly turn near Idgah circle. After which there was a situation of stoning and confrontation between the mobs of both communities... the Madhavpura police have lodged complaints of rioting against the mobs of both communities...

> Clashes sparked by personal altercation: Last night, a youth named Allahbraksha stood near the Madhavpura Idgah circle selling cassettes on a cart when Dinesh alias Dhoni Nadiya came there to buy cassettes. After an altercation over buying cassettes, mobs of both communities confronted each other. The police filed a complaint of rioting against the mobs.

Unlike the police report, these reports name the individuals involved in the "personal altercation" by publishing their identifiably Hindu and Muslim names. But this additional information does nothing to challenge the police view of the minor and the major. The actors may have names now, and the report mentions an altercation over the purchase of a music cassette, but they are still minor elements of a larger drama. They are merely inciting incidents and actors that led to the Event.

There are differences in how various Gujarati newspaper reports describe the incident. For instance, newspapers use different words—*dhamaal* or *toofan*—to name the violence. Some mention the number of tear gas shells ("more than two dozen") used by the police to quell the violence. But what is relevant for my argument here is the place of the minor in these articles. Mainstream newspaper reports don't disturb the fixed place of the minor that is key to the making of the communal riot in both the colonial and postcolonial archive. Lest one thinks that this kind of reporting is simply vernacular bias, here is a report published in the English newspaper *DNA* (*Daily News and Analysis*) on May 2, 2011:

MADHAVPURA WITNESSES FRESH COMMUNAL CLASHES

Following a violent scuffle between two communities late on Saturday night in Madhavpura, fresh violence was reported on Sunday evening as well. The irate mob took over the Idgah circle and started pelting stones at each other, set couple of vehicles on fire and vandalized several shops in the vicinity.... On Saturday the communities had clashed with each other at the Idgah circle over a *minor* monetary dispute. Both the groups had then pelted stones and vandalized shops.

The violence on Saturday was a fall out between two groups of people. Police said between 11:30 p.m. and 12 a.m. on Saturday, a group of four to five people approached a roadside vendor, Allabraksha, selling cassettes at Idgah circle. The group reportedly picked up a couple of cassettes but refused to pay for the same leading to a verbal fight, Madhavpura police. Later on, sources said, the group returned with a few more people and began arguing with the vendor. In response, another group supporting the vendor also gathered and in no time, the argument turned violent.

This is the most detailed newspaper report. The minor surfaces in it as a monetary dispute. But *why* did one "group of people" *refuse* to pay? In some way, the answer to that question is at the heart of the story. The seamless movement from the minor to the major in colonial accounts, the police FIRs, and mainstream newspaper reports is the move that is at stake here.

To be clear, the minor is not erased or repressed. It cannot be erased because then the whole scene of violence would become meaningless. Rather, it is the catalyst that transforms violence into myth.

"Making a Big Thing . . . Out of a Criminal Incident"

Intrigued by comments about Dhoni's role in the violence, I tried to meet more people in the neighborhood. Most Muslims lived in small one- or two-room tenements under a flyover. Some houses had an auto rickshaw parked outside them, a common form of self-employment and livelihood for many young Muslim men in Ahmedabad. Women who could afford to buy sewing machines and learn the basics worked from home. Like elsewhere in Ahmedabad, the streets were dotted with teashops usually surrounded by small groups of men (and their parked scooters and motorcycles) chatting, snacking, and reading a shared newspaper.

Because the violence was still fresh when I got there, the streets were empty and quiet. I noticed people staring at us as we drove through this usually bustling neighborhood. I was on a motorbike with Bharatbhai, who had been visiting this neighborhood for over a decade. Near one of the teashops, we met and chatted with a young Muslim man named Shafi. After exchanging greetings, the conversation turned to the recent events:

M: What's been happening?

SHAFI: Well, you see Dhoni—a local hoodlum—came to buy a cassette here and refused to pay the vendor. Since the guy who sells the cassettes was an outsider, not from this area, he beat him up. He did that only because he didn't know Dhoni. . . . Dhoni and his brother came back with more people to beat the vendor up and started creating trouble—damaging shops and fighting with people. Soon, the cassette vendor also got his friends from Dariapur (a nearby predominantly Muslim neighborhood) to fight Dhoni's boys. At some point, the vendor and his boys came running into our neighborhood shouting and screaming for help. . . . That's when the stoning started.

M: Who is this Dhoni guy anyway?

SHAFI: Dhoni collects *hafta* [extortion money] from the market in Prem Darwaja area. He is from a family of waste collectors [ex-untouchable caste]. Everyone knows this big shot's mother and sister still go out every day in the morning to pick waste from the streets. But he is powerful, he once threatened the mayor. . . . He is a charge-sheeter [he is an accused in cases relating to anti-Muslim violence in 2002]. I think these [Muslim] shops here don't give him "protection money" and once when he tried to forcibly collect money, Muslim shopkeepers beat him up. This area, especially the Muslim part is not yielding results for him.

Strongmen and local criminals are common across poor neighborhoods in India and have been described as "sovereigns beyond the state."[20] In his study of Hindu nationalist groups in Maharashtra, Hansen writes that the everyday violent performances of masculinity and authority by such strongman ("dada") figures competes with parallel formal authorities like the police and the bureaucracy. These figures demonstrate, according to Hansen, the dispersed structure of sovereignty in India.

Understood within the frame of vernacular performances of sovereignty, the "personal altercation" between Dhoni and the Muslim vendor is more than a faceoff between a "Hindu" and a "Muslim." Shafi's pointed comments about Dhoni's lower-caste status as a Dalit both deflates his performance of authority as a strongman and shows that the category "Hindu" is fractured here by caste. Dhoni is a local criminal with an elaborate extortion and (illegal) liquor business in the area. While newspapers and official documents describe this place as "riot-prone," referring to volatile Hindu-Muslim relations, this is also one of those rare neighborhoods in the city that is mixed. In a city where over 70 percent of neighborhoods are only populated by members of a single religious community, here Hindus and Muslims live beside each other, whether they want to or not. Dhoni Nadiya, the man who refused to pay, is well known to the police and politicians, but he is also well known to Muslims as a member of the Dalit community. Shafi's comments reiterate the point that religious animosity between Hindus and Muslims may not be the most relevant lens through which to understand the violent incident. Shafi's narrative *begins* not within the plot of the communal riot but in an everyday world that includes extortion, political and police patronage of criminal activity, caste politics, and the political economy of illegal liquor. He also begins with a character, not a trigger. Most importantly, Shafi's narrative upsets the relationship between the major and the minor elements to understand the incident. Note that many of the elements mentioned by Shafi are also within the newspaper reports in English and Gujarati (one *Times of India* article mentions that the police have arrested Dhoni and his gang members), but their minor status allows police reports and mainstream media to focus on the "eternal" animosity between Hindus and Muslims.

Focusing on "what everyone knows," we get a network of actors that involves gambling, illicit liquor, local policemen, and politicians. The dispute is both the refusal to pay for something and the later effort by Dhoni to teach the vendor a "lesson" for not respecting Dhoni's authority, which itself is on shaky grounds owing both to his low caste status and the fact that the Muslim neighborhood does not give him "protection" money. That's why Shafi needs to emphasize that the vendor was from outside, did not know Dhoni, and dared to not only ask for money but also beat him publicly when he refused. The political economy of illicit liquor and extortion, the performance of street-level masculinity, and a competition to control an area—any one of these threads or a combination of them would be as meaningful as the idea of Hindus and Muslims attacking each other after a minor altercation.

What I am calling here minor elements—the making and unmaking of everyday authority and the political economy of illicit liquor and gambling—do appear in newspaper reports of violence in Madhavpura that do not mention "communal clash." In 2015, The *Times of India* reported the death of a Muslim man in "rioting" in Madhavpura in which he was shot by the police during a women-led raid on the gambling and liquor dens in the area. Two years later, another newspaper, DNA, reported that a police inspector was suspended in Madhavpura for not acting against gambling and liquor in his jurisdiction. In fact, the newspaper report suggests that this economy is resented by *both* Hindus and Muslims in the area but patronized by the police. These reports are not simply embellishments to an existing narrative of religious animosity but are capable of producing their own story. As we passed a small bakery, a trustee of the Idgah mosque named Masoom waved us down for a cup of tea. For the most part, Masoom repeated Shafi's story about the role of Dhoni and his gang, but he was willing to go further and *name* the violence, and give a minor reading.

MASOOM: This is not a communal riot. We don't pay Dhoni extortion money, so he tries to threaten us. . . . This is a situation of Muslims against criminal elements. Unlike the situation in 2002 when all the Hindus came out on the streets, this time only Dhoni and his boys came out. Hindus did not come out to fight. It's a good sign for society that common people are not coming to join this violence. It's just the police. They are making it a communal riot—a big thing out of a criminal incident.

If we interpret "the big thing" as the making of majorities and minorities, what Masoom is alerting us is to the minor as the map of the everyday criminality, policing, extortion, and bootlegging that affects the lives of Muslims and Hindus. Masoom's comment goes to the heart of the puzzle that I encountered as I tried to make sense of what I read, heard, and saw in Madhavpura: two contrasting, even conflicting, compositions of violence, and yet one of them, the master narrative, circulated much more widely in mainstream media and public culture. If one of them locates power and agency with the community—Hindus and Muslims—the minor composition emphasizes the porous borders between the legal and the illegal and focuses on the role of police in framing criminal violence as communal violence. Not only is it not a war between Hindus and Muslims but the incident is also a failed attempt by criminals, Dhoni and his gang, to mobilize people in Madhavpura as Hindus. And yet this failed attempt at the level of the neighborhood nevertheless circulates outside as another incidence of communal violence that confirms its status as "riot-prone." One newspaper report, published in the *Times of India* on May 3, 2011, mentions that "the police cautioned the residents from making it a new hotspot for communal tension." And yet if we follow the minor perspective, it seems that it is not the residents but the police who have the power to make minor incidents major.

Focusing on the Minor

I returned to Madhavpura again after things had cooled down. There was a small blue tent in the middle of the traffic circle, indicating that the police had set up a makeshift Special Reserve Police (SRP) point at site of violence. The people had returned to the teashops. Everything looked normal. Still confused about the incidents that happened here a few weeks ago, I tried to meet the actors involved in the "personal altercation." I tried to meet Dhoni but had no success. I found out that it is not easy to meet a bootlegger without the right contacts. People would point to shuttered shops and decrepit buildings inside narrow lanes as illegal liquor dens, but they also said that I would never find him there. Especially not now when things were hot.

I also tried to find the young Muslim man who was selling cassettes that day. People said he no longer sold cassettes; some said he had left Gujarat after the violence to escape the police; and others like Shafi said he was never from this neighborhood. When everything failed, I tried a more indirect approach.

I met Aasim, a self-appointed leader of one of the Muslim-majority neighborhoods, talkative and helpful, with a keen interest in politics and gossip. Further, and this is key, he apparently ran an illegal gambling den and was respected by people because of his contacts with the police and criminal elements. He agreed to meet me in his wastepaper recycling shop under the Idgah flyover. It was a ten-minute walk from his shop to J's water shop.

Predictably, as soon as I mentioned the clashes, he got excited; like everyone else he blamed "Dhoni and his boys." As chance would have it, he was at the scene of violence that day, listening to music on his phone and enjoying a cup of tea, waiting to leave for the railway station to catch a late-night train. At some point, he saw Dhoni (whom he has known for many years now) with a couple of boys walking around with swords.

"Stop this drama and go home" he told Dhoni. To which Dhoni replied that someone had hit him at this spot and he must retaliate. People knew that there had been a scuffle between him and a vendor earlier in the day, and everyone thought it had ended there, but Dhoni came back with a gang of boys. He gathered them not very far away from the crossroads and even tried to persuade nearby Hindus to join them, but they refused. Then, they came here and burned shops and clashed with a group of Muslim boys who had assembled here by then.

In the middle of our conversation, Aasim suddenly made a phone call. "Someone wants to talk to you, come here for a bit?" After a few minutes, a thin young man with shiny slicked-back hair dressed in tight jeans showed up at the shop. He sat guardedly at the edge of the cot and looked warily at my bag and open notebook. Aasim introduced me as part of an NGO that was helping Muslim survivors of the 2002 violence. "He has come to understand what happened between you and Dhoni," he said.

The young man was none other than Allahbraksha, the vendor mentioned in all the newspaper reports. Initially he didn't talk and answered only in monosyllables but soon realized that I was only asking for information that "everyone knew."

That evening, like every evening, I was at my cart selling music cassettes at the crossroad. Dhoni and his friend M [the son of a nearby teashop owner] came and stood next to my cart. Then another guy came in a car and joined them. Dhoni asked me to give him twelve or thirteen cassettes, which I selected for him. Like, you know, the latest hits. Then Dhoni gave them to his friend in the car who drove away.

Since Dhoni and his friend were still there, I didn't ask their friend in the car for money, but when they started leaving, I asked for my money [30 rupees for each cassette]. His friend grabbed me and said, "Don't you know *him*?" "I know him very well" I said, "He may be a big man [*dada*] in his area, but I have a business to run, which means I buy these cassettes from the market and sell them for a profit." They pulled a knife on me and tried to fight me, but thankfully my friends were around, and we gave them a thrashing. The next day he came with twenty-five to thirty boys armed with sticks and swords. A police jeep stood and watched them without doing anything. Some boys from the other side [Muslim] also came, and then both groups started pelting stones at each other.

The most striking aspect of this account is the lack of spontaneity. The so-called Hindu-Muslim clash of "mobs of 500 each" was not an eruption of religious passion. There was a difference of a whole day between the minor incident and the major event, which unravels the idea of spontaneous violence between two religious communities. Second, the ostensibly minor incident is not the beginning but is already implicated in a larger story of police, criminals, and authority. The key character in the incident is not an anonymous Hindu but an identifiable strongman. By focusing on the minor, we also get a sense of the intimacy between neighbors even though mainstream reports seek to frame the two communities as separate except when they fight with each other. Both Aasim and Allahbraksha emphasized that the "police just stood and watched the armed men." Like the pogrom in 2002, the police inscribed targeted violence against Muslims as ethnic violence and were key actors in the performance of the violence.

My point is not to compare different narratives of violence to privilege the victims' version of events over official sources, or to poke holes in official narratives of violence. Rather, it is to point to the specific arrangement of major and minor elements that produces the illusion that every riot is the same as the one that happened before and will happen in the future.

A Minor Public

On May 3, 2011, the Muslim-owned newspaper *Gujarat Today* devoted a full page to the violence in Madhavpura. The headline of the main article ("Idgah Storm Not Communal but a Criminal Attack on Muslims") described "bootleggers and gangsters" attacking Muslim property causing losses of

ચોક્કસ તત્ત્વોના ઈશારે આયોજનબદ્ધ રીતે મુસ્લિમોને પાયમાલ કરવાનું ષડયંત્ર

ઈદગાહનું તોફાન કોમી નહીં પરંતુ ગુંડા તત્ત્વોનો મુસ્લિમો ઉપર હુમલો

દારૂના બુટલેગરો અને ગુંડા તત્ત્વો ચોક્કસ સમયે મારક હથિયારો સાથે અલગ અલગ દિશાઓમાંથી નીકળ્યા અને મુસ્લિમોની માલ-મિલકતોને લાખોનું નુકસાન પહોંચાડ્યું

તોફાની તત્ત્વોએ વેરેલ વિનાશ અને આગ બાદ ભંગારમાં ફેરવાઈ ગયેલ વાહનો તથા અન્ય ચીજ વસ્તુઓ

1.1 "Idgah incident not communal but a criminal attack on Muslims" headline of *Gujarat Today* article on May 3, 2011.

millions. It quoted Jafar saying that when he approached the police, they asked him "why had he kept his shop open" even when he told them that the Hindu mob broke into his shop and burned it down. Inside the main article, there were direct quotations from Muslim witnesses. "Seeing the gangsters not getting support from peaceful Hindu people, the Muslims maintained restraint despite huge loss to property." As a Muslim-owned daily newspaper with a large Muslim readership, *Gujarat Today*, unlike mainstream newspapers, broke away from the mainstream news reporting in 2002 as well. This gives us a sense of what it may take to make a minor public. At one level it seems that this flies against my argument that the minor reading fails to take off and reach a wider public. The point here is that *Gujarat Today* is known as a Muslim newspaper. Not only is it not readily available in most newsstands, unlike the other newspapers, but it largely circulates within a minor public comprising mainly Muslims.

What does a minor reading offer us? First, it helps us understand how and why violence against minorities is rendered unremarkable, an affliction of "riot-prone" neighborhoods and the communities who live inside them. It shows how public knowledge about so-called religious violence absolves the state, especially the police, as the key author of the idea of Hindus and Muslims as homogenous communities that think and act like warring races. Second, as the form of the riot jumps from the police report to public discourse via the newspaper, it produces a world of timeless, endless religious enmity. It closes doors to developing and circulating minor readings that refuse the colonial logic of Hindus and Muslims as perpetual enemies. Third, it helps us understand that struggles over what constitutes public information and official knowledge about violence is a struggle between the major and the minor. To understand this struggle, I have offered a form of surface reading[21] that tracks the minor, describes it, opens it up, and uses it like a sharp edge to understand the process of minoritization. To do a minor reading of violence means asking why certain forms move along and others do not.[22] It means identifying elements that transform violence into myth. What moves the master narrative along then is not simply the power of the police, even if that is true and obvious, but rather the inextricability of mainstream news reportage from police writing.

The major is not simply the brute power of the state to obfuscate but the ability of what Veena Das calls the "signature of the state" to circulate within disparate publics.[23] In circulation, the formation of Hindus and Muslims through violence is no longer the voice of the police but is simply public information. By taking seriously the ability of police writing to break away from its strict juridical field and attach itself to wider contexts, by tracking the iterability of the major-minor relationship in newspaper reports, we see the role of news-making and police reports in constituting a timeless world of Hindus versus Muslims. This is both more and less than the straightforward erasure of anti-Muslim violence. A minor reading shows that master narratives may not need to rely on erasure and repression. Within the master narrative and its desire to narrate violence as repetition, the minor remains on the surface—the minor altercation, the minor incident, the minor characters, that which requires no explanation. The minor also appears as that which is inexplicable within the logic of the major (if the rioting is about the spontaneous outburst of religious animosity, then why is there a lag of a day between the personal altercation and collective violence). The example of *Gujarat Today* illustrates that there is always the possibility of disturbing the relationship between the major and the minor to forge a counter-public, a counternarrative.

To read police and newspaper reports beside each other gives us a sense of the legal beyond the question of legal culpability, beyond who is tried and who escapes the law. The law is hardly impotent, corrupt, or lazy. Rather, the law as police writing inserts itself across scales (local and national, English and vernacular), whereby even disparate scenes of everyday violence (*toofan* and *dhamaal*) are transformed into a colonial framework of "riot-prone" spaces. By focusing on "what everyone knows" as well as minor elements on the surface of police and newspaper reports, I have presented a legal-media writing machine that fashions Indian society in terms of *ethnic difference*. A form of world-making that is continuously producing a public sphere of Hindus and Muslims at war with each other.

Composing the Archive

ON MARCH 25, 2002, a month into the statewide anti-Muslim violence, the *Times of India* reported that:

> The riot victims may feel they are on the path to getting justice by having filed the FIR [police First Information Report], but as advocates helping some of the victims are realizing, the police may have skillfully manipulated many of the FIRs to ensure that the accused go scot free. All they have to do is accuse a faceless mob of violence, effectively ensuring that the FIR ends up as just another piece of paper.

Consider three examples of what happened when Muslims tried to file a police complaint. When Baradkhan, a resident of Ida village went to the police station to file a report, the policemen told him that the *sarpanch* (headman) had already filed an "omnibus" report (a collective report with no details of specific incidents and accused) for all Muslims in the village and therefore no separate report was needed. Abbas bhai in Sinol village tried twice to file a police report against the men who burned his house. The police refused to file a complaint with the names of the accused. They would either file a complaint against a nameless mob or not file a complaint at all. Bazi, a Muslim businessman, saw his garage looted and burned by his Hindu neighbors in front of his eyes. His neighbor brought a truck to transport the looted items. When Bazi approached the police station, the officers shunted him away saying there were too many people waiting before him to get their complaints registered. Three days later, when he returned to the police station in the morning, the policemen wrote a rough (*kacchi*) report (not an FIR) and didn't give him a copy. A few weeks later, officers from the Crime Branch finally took his statement, prepared a seizure report (*panchnama*), and gave him a copy of his complaint. This was a rare achievement. He was one of very few Muslims who managed to file a police complaint that mentioned the names of Hindu accused in it.

The police FIR is the first step in the criminal justice system in India. It derives its legal authority from Section 154 (1) of the Indian Code of Criminal Procedure, 1973. It is the key moment when a "cognizable offence" given orally by a complainant is "reduced to writing" by a police officer. As the opening vignettes suggest, this black-letter description of the FIR is quite different from the reality of police documentation in India. Even though the FIR is a malleable document (it can be amended and quashed and challenged by the petitioner, judge, prosecution, and defense), it is supposed to record the "basic facts" surrounding an offense. The fact that it is preliminary and basic does not mean it is unimportant. The Supreme Court of India has declared that the FIR is the "basis of the case set up by the informant. It is an extremely vital and valuable piece of evidence for the purpose of corroborating the oral evidence adduced at the trial and can hardly be overestimated from the standpoint of the accused."[1]

Activists and scholars have documented the fact that for subalterns the experience of filing a police complaint in India is never straightforward. The partisan role of the Gujarat police is hardly shocking in the Indian context where police authority is always provisional because it is predicated on numerous external factors, including political patronage.[2] In fact, the Indian bureaucracy's obsession with paperwork is better understood as a form of structural state violence on the poor and the illiterate.[3] Indeed, Akhil Gupta argues that such practices "without appearing to be biased in any manner, the emphasis on what was written in a file, therefore, sometimes helped perpetuate structural violence on the poor."[4] Even in ordinary times, state officials use writing to erase their actions and operate in what Aradhana Sharma calls "mode of erasure."[5] From day one of the attacks on Muslims, the partisan nature of police action was clear from newspaper reports that described the police looking away as Hindu mobs destroyed Muslim property and life. Police bias against Muslims cemented rather than undermined their authority. *The Hindu* reported on May 17, 2002, that when senior policemen suspended a police inspector in Ahmedabad for inaction in protecting

Muslims during the rioting, the people of the neighborhood (presumably Hindus) observed a daylong *bandh* (shutdown) in protest. In other words, police inaction may have been illegal and morally objectionable but was socially approved by the wider public. In this context, it is not surprising to learn that the police resisted filing complaints against Hindus and acted as a partisan force to teach Muslims a lesson.

And yet the focus of much scholarly and activist literature is to expose the partisan role of the police in reporting and archiving violence. This brings us to a familiar approach in analyzing archives of violence: expose the epistemic violence of state documentary practices. This mode of reading the archive produces its own genre of human rights and civil society fact-finding reports that describe the police's refusal to register complaints against the majority Hindu community as the failure of the rule of law. If we take this well-worn path, we reach a familiar place—archives as one more sign of state violence. But this story fails to consider relationships between archives and violence that cannot be captured within binaries of absence and presence, erasure and repression, revelation and secrecy. I noticed the inadequacy of these binaries for reading archives of violence when I started noticing patterns *within* the police archive[6]—patterns that were generally neglected in the analysis of the archive since they did more than simply erase the violence. Minor forms like repetition, aggregation, and affect were on the surface of the police archive. They did not simply immunize state authorities from accountability but also comprised the archival infrastructure of antiminority violence itself. By infrastructure, I mean the forms of writing in the archive that outlive the bias of individual police officers and political regimes; police writing that transforms political violence against Muslims into religious conflict; and patterns that congealed, temporalized, and sequenced public violence so that it can be legally inscribed, discussed, and then dismissed. These forms of police reporting trafficked in affects and categories that draw on and proliferate a normative world, a *nomos*,[7] a world in which a large-scale public attack on minorities, especially Muslims, becomes part of a larger project of Hindu supremacist rule in India.

This is a project that surely did not start or end with the Gujarat pogrom but operates through the maintenance of minorities as collectives who can be routinely exposed to public violence, of which riots and pogroms are only one form.[8] What do we find within archives of violence if we turn our attention away from questions of erasure to questions of repetition? Like my reading of media accounts of violence in the previous chapter, I focus here on composing the archive based on what is aggregated and repeated and even left blank. A compositional reading that stays on the surface, observing the forms of time and space that constitute archives as a technology of antiminority violence.

To equate archives of violence with archives of destruction means that we continue to search for something left out, something to expose, to catch some new illegality, and draw yet another portrait of what Nietzsche called "the coldest of all cold monsters." State-centric perspectives on the archive make unreadable what lies beyond the legal/illegal. At the level of politics, this perspective is worn thin from overuse. Over the last decade, I have found myself grappling with the question: do I really need to uncover the prejudice of police archives during a pogrom? Who is really surprised to know that the same police that frequently helped Hindu mobs in attacking Muslims and even shot Muslims inside their homes did not impartially record the attack on them? This is not to undermine the importance of human rights projects that help us understand how the police treat minorities but to ask questions of archives that exceed the problem of erasure and repression.

I say this as I acknowledge that I did not approach the police archive on my own terms.[9] I encountered the archive sitting beside Justice First (JF) activists and lawyers in their meetings when they discussed legal cases, updated the program coordinators about the status of the cases they were handling, and discussed their legal strategy. Listening to discussions between lawyers and paralegals, I realized that the FIR—what was included and excluded from it—was the basis of most legal discussions. The police archive was clearly, in historian Kristin Weld's words, a "site for political struggle and contestation."[10] And yet the limits of this struggle in Gujarat, unlike the case in Guatemala where terror archives were repurposed for new ends, became quickly apparent to me. JF read police archives to expose the cunning of the Hindu nationalist state. Activists and lawyers pointed out that FIRs often falsified victims' testimonies, erased incidents of violence, and failed to mention key details and witnesses. In response, JF spent inordinate amounts of time collecting injury certificates, tallying what was included and excluded from police reports, correcting witnesses' statements, and sending Right to Information (RTI) applications to assemble a record of "what really happened." For activists, then, the police archive was an ember of violence past as well as a symbol of ongoing state impunity. This meant that the activist approach to the archive was to focus on its power to determine legal outcomes in ways that favored Hindus over Muslims.

I found that this important reading strategy (focused on exposure and erasure) missed the *forms* that lie on the surface of the archive—like aggregation, repetition, and affect. It was necessary to ask the archive of violence not only what does it destroy or preserve, but what does it have going for it, how does it persist, and what interrupts it? These are forms that connect the exceptional with the routine, the colonial to the postcolonial, through the force of repetition and difference.[11] This chapter is an outcome of my struggle to work with an archive that wears its politics on its sleeve. Annelise Riles suggests that in cases "where the 'norms' are not hidden but are excessively explicit and located on the surface, insistently posed and restated at every turn, the documents themselves may have different uses altogether, and so might the work of anthropological analysis."[12] This kind of work requires that we "seek to visualize the forms latent in the norms themselves."[13] Composing the archive thus entails a certain form of visualization, a seeing anew, that does not necessarily dig inside the document as much as notice its patterning, what Ann Stoler calls an "along the grain" reading.[14] This way of reading archives emphasizes densities, regularities, and distributions to pay attention to the materiality and ambiguity of the archive rather than simply use it to extract answers.[15]

Repetition: The Preface

Hindu nationalist groups like the VHP (World Hindu Council) as well as the Gujarat government described the attacks on Muslims as a "spontaneous" reaction to the Godhra incident. On the one hand, the riots were presented as an outburst of Hindu anger against Muslims, and on the other hand, the burning of the train and deaths of the Hindus in Godhra was described as a terrorist act. On February 28, 2002, Chief Minister Narendra Modi described the deaths of Hindus as a "pre-planned, violent act of terrorism." Later in an interview to a television channel, he infamously described the ongoing state-wide attacks on Muslims as "a chain of action and reaction." The head of the Hindu right-wing organization VHP was less circumspect and called the attack on Muslims a "befitting reply to what has been perpetrated on the Hindus in the last 1,000 years." This spontaneous theory of the riot found its way into the police archive in the form of a *preface*. A preface shared by all one hundred and eleven FIRs in the Madhavpura police station. This preface was repeated in police reports across Gujarat. So regardless of the accused, complainant, and time and place of the offense, the reports opened with these framing sentences:

> Due to the attack on *karsevaks* (Hindu nationalists) traveling on a train in Godhra yesterday on 27.02.2002, the VHP announced a *Bandh* [shutdown] on 28.02.2002 during which communal riots erupted in various parts of Ahmedabad . . .

At first glance this preface seems rather unremarkable. It seems like "mere" context. It describes the violence as an unmarked and unmotivated "eruption." What is remarkable here is that an apparently nondiscursive form of violence—rioting—is made possible by a discursive form—the preface.[16] These sentences are then repeated in police stations across Gujarat. This is also the linear time of the colonial communal riot.[17] Linear time here means that public rape, arson, looting, and stabbing becomes an effect of the death of Hindus. The preface *connects* dispersed acts of violence over several days and weeks across Gujarat into a meaningful narrative of the communal riot. What it achieves is basically the same thing that the head of the VHP, Pravin Togadia, said more bluntly: "wherever there will be a Godhra, there will be a Gujarat." In this way, the preface is the most compact discursive form that links the internal textual matter of disparate attacks on Muslims with Hindu nationalist discourse. Insofar as we see such prefaces repeated in descriptions of "riots" across India, it is also a portable narrative that bridges what is inside and outside the official archive. In this sense, the preface is paratext that allows the police (since they stitch these sentences to every report) to anchor their writing within wider narrative cartographies and affective geographies found in political speeches, newspaper reports, and official narratives.

It is noteworthy that the preface is *not* exceptional in the history of police reporting about antiminority pogroms. In the 1984 anti-Sikh riots, policemen in Delhi, India's capital, insisted on "dictating the framing sentences of the First Information Report." By doing so, they essentially framed the attacks on Sikhs as a spontaneous outburst of Hindu anger at the assassination of the then prime minister Indira Gandhi.[18] Veena Das analyzes such documentary strategies to show the double-edged power of documents to inscribe "the lie of the state."[19] Their double edge comes from the fact that the same police documents that misrepresented the pogrom against the Sikhs as a spontaneous riot were at the same time documentary proof that the Sikh complainant was a victim.

But my interest is not only the distance of the preface from the truth. I want to emphasize the availability of the preface within the Indian police archive of a form that lets police officers across Gujarat (and across India) stabilize the space–time of exceptional violence against minorities as mob violence. The iterability of such prefaces within the police archive across time and space—policemen deployed it in Delhi 1984 and Gujarat 2002—helps us locate the precise links that consolidate the riot not simply as a legal object but also as a narrative act.[20] The power of the preface is inseparable from its *repeatability* that, unlike what proceeds after it (the specifics of particular offenses), is mechanically reproduced across thousands of police reports without the stain of bias and illegality. As preface after preface describes what happened in Godhra as a "carnage" (*hatyakand*), the "burning alive of Hindu workers," and the "large-scale killing of Hindu nationalists," the archive stabilizes the political violence against Muslims as a spontaneous reaction of "Hindus" (also the language of the Hindu nationalists). It removes the "epistemic murk" around the "origin" of violence—the incident in Godhra.[21] Who burned the train, and how and why? Two different politically competing investigations of the burning of the train came to two different conclusions. The Gujarat government report established a Muslim conspiracy to attack Hindu nationalists, and a Ministry of Railways (headed by a rival political party's politician) report found that the burning of the S-6 coach of the train was an accident.

The sequencing of violence within the preface is also important because it connects the colonial to the postcolonial. Historian Gyan Pandey calls the narrative of a British colonial force restoring order to stop Hindus and Muslims from attacking each other as the "colonial master narrative of the communal riot."[22] At the level of the preface, little seems to have changed in terms of the postcolonial state's imagination of Hindus and Muslims permanently at war. The preface inserts the deaths of Hindus at Godhra into a temporal scheme that transforms disparate acts of arson, murder, stabbing, and looting into yet another riot between Hindus and Muslims. In the present, what is at stake is not so much the civilizing force of the colonial police to tame a savage colonized population as much as the power of repetition to normalize antiminority violence. Once you have a formula—Muslims *attack* Hindus on the train (trigger) + Hindus *versus* Muslims (reaction) = Communal Riot—that can be inserted into the preface of the police report, then what follows is foretold.

Over time, the mechanical reproduction of the preface, its absurdity, and its repetition in the police archive seem to simply mirror the sequence of events repeated on television, in newspapers, and in political speech. It is the affective thread that allows the police archive to join Hindu nationalist political speech, mainstream media, and the language of the state to frame antiminority violence as religious antagonism. While it is well known that the ability of the police to frame crimes in writing gives them significant power to shape legal outcomes, the preface tells us something about the force of repetition in the archive.

Aggregation: The Omnibus FIR

In a list prepared by JF on "victims' experience of registering an FIR," I noticed that the most common reason for the police to refuse to file a complaint was that an "omnibus FIR" had already been filed. *Omnibus* FIRs are reports that aggregate different incidents of violence in disparate neighborhoods by different actors over a seventy-two-hour period into a *single* complaint. Let us look at how the police filed such reports in Madhavpura. On March 3, 2002, four police sub-inspectors in four different police stations wrote separate yet identical reports. Each report covered offenses during the crucial seventy-two hours (February 28 to March 3) that comprised the bulk of the attacks against Muslims. During these three days, Hindu mobs shut down (*bandh*) public transportation and shops, took to the streets to "protest" the death of Hindus in Godhra, and when finally the army arrived, patrolled the streets, and buried the bodies, much of the killing had already happened. All four reports describe the ensuing rioting around their police stations as follows:

> I [name of police inspector] along with other members of the staff were patrolling the area around our *chowki* [police station] in the requisite vehicle during the Gujarat *Bandh* [shutdown] on the 28.02.2002, when several communal mobs with deadly weapons and explosive substances, numbering between 100 to 2,000 attacked, damaged, burned and destroyed the property, religious places, and households of residents at different places near the police station area causing heavy damages. To protect the life and property of people, the police after adequate warning resorted to *lathi* charge, tear gas, and firing.

An eruption of irrational communal violence as usual. A struggling police force trying to control rioting mobs that seem to appear and disappear out of nowhere. In response to such police reports, human rights activists, journalists, and survivors were quick to point out that these reports erased key facts like the role of organized Hindu nationalist activists and local politicians in leading and organizing the mobs, often with the support of the very policemen who later wrote these reports.

This rather capacious form of police writing allowed officers to combine and subsume incidents ranging from arson to murder by communal mobs (*sampradayik quomi todu*) of "unidentifiable persons numbering from 100 to 2,000." Also called "running FIRs" by the state administration, they cover disparate offenses across police stations but are identical except for the author (name of the inspector) and the number of accused (the size of the mob).[23]

Put differently, the police were able to absorb the most violent phase of the attacks on Muslims within the archive without documenting anything at all using the omnibus form. Inside the omnibus report, there are no specific details of any incident, no individuals are identified, no weapons are recovered, no arrests are made, and no witnesses are mentioned. At the same time, because of the first-ness of these reports and their ability to cover large swathes of time and space, when Muslim survivors came to the police to file their complaints, the police told them that they were already included within the omnibus FIR and there was no need for them to file separate complaints. What we find here is a police strategy of aggregation that lies on the surface of the archive.

During JF legal meetings and documentation, many omnibus cases came up for discussion, and when these cases came up for trial, JF repeated a well-known fact about criminal trials: there is no possibility of prosecution without the evidence of *specific* crimes by *specific* individuals. As a lawyer once told me, no judge could hold a "mob of unidentifiable persons numbering between 100–2000" guilty. In the omnibus FIR there are no individuals, individual agency, or specific targets; the mostly Muslim shops, vehicles, businesses, religious places, and houses are unmarked. Not actors but affect is the accused. Unknown mobs are the *agents* of violence, but they are agents in the form of a nondiscursive entity like a storm or a fire, and they destroy the "property, religious places, and households" of unidentified "residents." Only if you read eyewitness testimony, human rights reports, and FIRs registered by victims many days (and sometimes months) *after* the incident does it become clear that most "religious places" were Muslim shrines (*dargahs*) and mosques, and the "property and households" destroyed are also mostly Muslim-owned.

Activists argued that this practice of writing omnibus FIRs was illegal. Beyond the question of legality, however, is the question of form. What does this aggregative form produce? How do we understand the affordances of the omnibus report? Is it an aberration that was only practiced by the Gujarat police in 2002? It turns out, like the preface, the omnibus FIR is *not* an invention of the Gujarat police and is certainly not an exceptional strategy to respond to a state of emergency. The omnibus report is an expansion and intensification of existing police archival forms and reporting practices, at hand during events of collective violence. For instance, human rights lawyer and scholar Vrinda Grover argues that in filing omnibus FIRs the Gujarat police acted according to a "familiar pattern" first noticed in the anti-Sikh violence in Delhi 1984:

> As in Delhi 1984, the police adopted an innovative and illegal method of registering FIRs. Instead of registering a separate and distinct FIR about each cognizable offense, a single omnibus FIR is recorded. The contents are general, vague, and bereft of details. The incidents reported therein relate to different places, time and accused persons. . . . Such FIRs will ensure that the investigations and prosecution of criminal offences would be no more than an exercise in futility.[24]

The omnibus FIR has received extensive attention from activists for what it excludes from the archive—witness testimony. Arvind Narrain argues that this erasure allows the omnibus FIRs to "construct 'partial' truths because they do not include the victims' perspective, and do not mention the motivation behind the violence, hence making the violence random."[25] Further, "the legal truth of the FIR elided the significant question of naming the accused and instead produced the anonymous figure of the mob."[26] Both Grover and Narrain point out the power of the FIR to produce the rioting mob by erasing key details. My point is that this key effect of the FIR is produced through not simply erasure but also aggregation. This inseparability of aggregation as positivity and erasure as negativity in the same document becomes clear when we realize that even as the omnibus report erases individuals and agency, it mobilizes affects like anger to explain the appearance of mobs. The aggregation of individuals into mobs and then mobs into Hindus and Muslims signifies a communal mood. The rioting mob stands in for an angry and hurt Hindu public. I want to emphasize here that we notice two orders of repetition: the repetition of the omnibus FIR within Gujarat and the repetition of the "omnibus form" across India.

Blanks

Imagine the first three days of the pogrom. The VHP (World Hindu Council) declares a *bandh* that *unofficially* shuts down the city and clears the streets: shops, businesses and offices are closed. This unofficial shutdown is supported by the ruling Hindu nationalist government, making it effectively an official shutdown. Now that the streets are empty of the flow of everyday life, rioting "erupts" in different parts of the city. Fearing violence, residents of the city do not open their shops and businesses and stay back at home. As Hindu mobs take over the city, the government and police impose a curfew. Now, no one is *officially* allowed to step outside their house, and yet the streets are throbbing with rioters. Amidst these multiple shutdowns, official and unofficial, Hindu mobs, often under the supervision of the police, proceed to meticulously destroy Muslim tombs, factories, shops, and neighborhoods. The *bandh*—public announcement by a political group to shut down a city—is a common technique of agitation in India. Within the police archive, however, it produces a kind of temporality that attempts to shut down legal witnessing.

The legal (curfew) and the licit (*bandh*) produce a space–time in which there can be no legitimate witnessing of violence because simply being present would be already to violate the law. Imagine this situation from the perspective of Muslims. How can they see the destruction of their life and property and not at the same time implicate themselves as rioters? Here the time-space of the *bandh* is the agent of destruction itself. Not simply because this time is illegal or is yet more "evidence of state complicity," as human rights reports describe it, but the *bandh* acts as the conditions of possibility for public violence against minorities. But that is not all. It also makes its witnessing suspect before the judge. After all, anyone who claims to have witnessed the destruction of their shop could be accused of being a rioter for breaking the curfew. For instance, a Hindu defense lawyer during the cross-examination of a Muslim witness (a shopkeeper who reported seeing his Hindu neighbors burn down his shop) suggested that perhaps his fellow Muslim shopkeepers destroyed his shop out of jealousy.

After the first spate of police-authored omnibus reports, from March 7 onward, most reports in the police archive are from Muslim shopkeepers and caretakers of religious properties. In these reports, sometimes the police simply leave the space given for writing the names of the accused blank. These blanks in turn mirror the larger blankness of the archive itself, which is after all empty in terms of subjectivity. How do we read these blanks?

What if they are not simply acts of state violence but constitute the space–time of antiminority violence? In other words, I use the blankness of certain police reports to show the entanglement between forms of violence and forms of writing. Together, they constitute a blank but public space and time to attack minorities.

Time here is not univocal. If the preface of the FIR uses linear time to frame targeted antiminority violence as a riot, then there is another form of time that admits no witnesses. Before I describe the contours of this time, consider one estimate of the physical destruction that took place in the seventy-two hours or three days of the *bandh* (shutdown): "10,000 shops, businesses, factories, and vendor carts" were destroyed and "rough estimates of economic losses" suggest a 600-crore (6 billion USD) loss to the hotel industry; 230 mosques, *dargahs* (shrines) and *mazhars* were damaged in the first seventy-two hours.[27]

It may be surprising to learn that this mass destruction of mostly Muslim commercial, residential, and religious property was in fact recorded by the police. And it constitutes the bulk of the police archive. More than half of the total FIRs (fifty-one out of 111) in the Madhavpura police station are simply lists of materials and machinery destroyed and looted by the mobs, including estimates of the financial loss incurred as well. Like the omnibus FIR, except the name of the complainant and the material details of physical destruction, these reports are almost identical and read as follows:

When the VHP announced a Gujarat Bandh on the 28.02.2002, *I did not open my restaurant and stayed home during the Bandh.* During the Bandh, communal riots erupted in different parts of Ahmedabad city and communal mobs indulged in stone throwing and arson with explosive substances because of which *curfew was imposed on the city. Because of which I did not go to my restaurant and stayed at home,* and only found out late at night that during the Bandh on the 28.02.2002 communal mobs of 2000 or more threw stones, looted and burned my restaurant. *Because of the curfew* and the tense conditions prevailing at the time, I did not go to my restaurant till the 4th March…. (emphasis mine)

Notice that the space–time of this report is very different from the temporality of the omnibus FIR and the preface. Fearing violence during the shutdown, most Muslims stayed away from their businesses. Many fled to safer areas: relief camps, relatives' houses, and neighboring Muslim majority neighborhoods. When they returned home or checked on their shops and businesses *after* the three-day shutdown, they found their houses, businesses, and shops looted or burned down. Therefore, regardless of whether the property destroyed is a restaurant, shop, warehouse, or religious structure, the police report uses the shutdown to prepare a template: *bandh* → complainant absent from the scene of offense → no accused or witness. So here we have a third type of repetition in the police archive.

In this sense, *bandh* time is more than simply an illegality that receives government sanction. Paul Brass argues that the police curfew is more a "means of control, victimization, and outright violence against targeted groups rather than as devices to bring peace for the benefit of all."[28] Reading the form of anti-Muslim violence from inside the FIR shows that it produces a punctuated temporality inside and outside the archive to absorb recurrent antiminority violence in India. This, in turn, helps us understand the recurrence of these temporalities of antiminority violence across South Asia and beyond. Together, the unofficial *bandh* and its official counterpart of the curfew—when the police and the administration impose emergency restrictions on the movement of people and goods—create a space–time in which mass violence becomes *natural* destruction: anonymous violence without agency and legal culpability.

To see the starkness of these reports, we need to step outside the police archive for a moment. On the day of the *bandh*, anthropologist Parvis Ghassem-Fachandi saw policemen smoking cigarettes with their backs to the rampage, even as "cars are set on fire" and "youths with orange headbands" (typically worn by far-right Hindu groups) enforced the *bandh* by closing shops and preventing commuters from going to work. The police watched all this from the comfort of a tent that gave them shade from the sun. Ghassem-Fachandi watched "a group of ten policemen with water jugs, their rifles leisurely leaning against a brick wall." They watched a group 50–100 youngsters burn cars in the middle of the street. Children helped these youths, bringing "stones, bricks, plates and iron rods." Viewing these scenes from inside the police archive, we understand why the perpetrators wear "neither masks nor helmets."[29]

"Hurting the Feelings of Hindus"

What happens if we read the difference in how police inscribed violence against Hindus and Muslims not through content but form? Not through what is erased but through the feelings ascribed to Hindus and Muslims? By reading the affects that anchor the movement and actions of the mob, we see that the FIR summons and reinforces peculiar types of collectivities named Hindus and Muslims. In terms of affect, the FIR follows the familiar colonial template of the communal riot—the spontaneous eruption of sectarian violence between Hindus and Muslims. But something different happens when Muslims appear in these reports as perpetrators. On March 28, 2002, a Hindu man registered a FIR about his brother's murder. The next day a Muslim man registered a FIR about his brother's murder. But the reports read quite differently (emphasis mine):

1   Due to the attack on Hindu nationalist activists [*karsevaks*] in Godhra on the 27.02.2002, the VHP announced a Gujarat *Bandh* and the city was tense.... The people next door informed me that my brother fled the municipal quarters when *a mob of about 100 Muslims gathered*... then suddenly a car appeared whose number I don't know, and some *Muslims emerged from the car with daggers and swords* and murdered him. At which time the police dispersed the mob with tear gas shells and firing. At present I do not know the name of the *Muslims*.

2   Due to the attack on Hindu nationalist activists [*karsevaks*] in Godhra on the 27.02.2002, the VHP announced a Gujarat *Bandh* and the city was tense.... I along with all my brothers went to stay at my uncle's house. Because we left behind our 5 goats and 8 hens, my brother went back at 8 a.m. to feed them. When he did not return quickly, our neighbors informed us that near Ishwarnagar a *mob of 15–20 unidentified men* burned and murdered my brother. Out of fear we did not step out but went straight to identify the body in the civil hospital.

Both reports share the common preface about the attack on Hindu nationalist activists, the tension caused by the *bandh*, and the eruption of rioting. In both cases, the complainants are not eyewitnesses but hear about the murder from others. In both cases, a mob commits the murder. But notice that when the complainant is a Hindu, the murder is not random. It is a "mob of about 100 Muslims." The murder of the Hindu man is detailed: the weapons ("swords and daggers") used by the perpetrators and the precise mode of their entry and escape are described. In other words, we have moved away from the blankness of the archive; the Muslims are organized, motivated, and armed. In contrast, the death of the Muslim man is an anonymous murder by "unidentified men." The perpetrator's identity is unnamed, which leaves it open for defense lawyers to suggest, as they did in a different court case, that perhaps "Muslims attacked each other."

This shift is most perceptible during the last phase of the pogrom, when the police no longer file omnibus and blank reports. From March 15 onward, the police write reports *naming* Muslims. This shift in pattern, according to one human rights report, coincides with the mass arrest of Muslims who tried to protect their neighborhoods from Hindu mobs. I want to note here that, until this phase, the police did *not* write the name of the accused and neither did they arrest anyone at the scene of the violence. But something different starts happening when the Muslim appears as an agent in the archive.

Now, we find three FIRs in the police archive, two of which specifically *name* Muslims as the accused. The FIR is no longer an inventory of anonymous destruction by sectarian mobs but frames the Muslim as a minority hurting the feelings of the majority. It draws on a larger affective map of Hindu nationalist attempts to construct Hinduism as a majoritarian religion that stretches all the way back to events like the 1992 destruction of the Babri Mosque and VHP-organized events in faraway places like Ayodhya. The last phase of FIRs is best understood against this backdrop of Hindu nationalist performances of Hinduism as a public religion under attack from minorities like Muslims.

Ayodhya, a Hindu pilgrim town in the northern Indian state of Uttar Pradesh, is the site where far-right Hindu groups destroyed a sixteenth-century mosque in 1992. They claimed that Muslims had built a mosque on the site of a temple that marked the birth of the popular Hindu deity Ram and started a movement to construct a new temple at the same site. The demolition and controversy over the ownership of temple and mosque was a matter of litigation and political agitation for the Hindu nationalist movement until the Supreme Court of India approved the construction of a temple at the site of the demolished mosque in 2019.

On March 15, 2002, the VHP organized a *shila daan* (ritual act of placing an idol in a temple) in Ayodhya that accompanied "religious" events in Ahmedabad. Newspapers in Ahmedabad reported that the "VHP performs *aarti* (prayers) in Ahmedabad for the success of *shila daan*." They also mentioned that "Ahmedabad too [along with Ayodhya] is tense. Hindu organizations have put up public notices urging the community to perform prayers and blow conch shells for the success of the *shila daan* programme in Ayodhya." Other contemporary reports also mentioned the "prayers" accompanied by the "blowing of conch shells" during the VHP-organized event.

Concurrent with these VHP events, police wrote reports describing a mob of "around 5,000 Muslims" using "provocative communal language that hurt Hindu sentiments that lead to a confrontation between the two communities." These reports string together "Muslims" with spaces like the "mosque" and objects like "swords, daggers, and pipes," and language like "Praise Allah" and "Kill! Chop!" The FIRs mention by name the neighborhoods from where Muslim mobs emerge and use "provocative words that hurt Hindu sentiment" (*hinduni lagni dubhay taevi quomi ushkaerni janak shabdo*). Why does it matter that the police inscribe violence against Muslims within an affective economy of Hindu hurt? Because the ability of police writing to inscribe disparate moods—from blankness to wounding—shows that the official archive is an affectively charged entity that can both reproduce a template and also create wounded majorities.

The Trace

No archive can close the circle. On March 9, the police registered five complaints (out of the total 111) identifying Hindus with their names. These FIRs interrupt the usual description of anonymous violence that has dominated the police archive so far. The five reports appear on the same day and are easy to miss because they are buried under the refrain of anonymous complaints. In the span of an hour, five Muslims who live in the same neighborhood (*chali*) registered complaints against their Hindu neighbors. They begin with the usual preface about the Godhra train incident but end on a very different note:

> I was at my garage at around 1 in the afternoon when 1. B. Thakore 2. R. Thakore 3. M. Thakore 4. N. Thakore 5. J. Thakore 6. V. Thakore 7. Amritlal, who is B. Thakore's son-in-law, and 8. Mahesh alias Tikko—all residing in BB colony, led a mob armed with swords and dagger of around 40 other persons with them.

Notice that the Hindus identified belong to the same family and caste. The accused and the complainant are *neighbors*, and the reports even identify kinship relations between the accused. The reports describe the accused as "5–6 boys from *our* colony." Suddenly, us versus them has transformed into intimate violence between neighbors. This trace in the archive points to what Shruti Kapila calls the fraternal nature of political violence in the Indian context; the violence is not between friends and enemies but between neighbors, brothers, and intimates. Tracing the origin of this form of intimate violence to the "civil war" of the Partition of India and Pakistan in 1947, Shruti Kapila writes, "The arrival of a Muslim nation as India's neighbor dramatically transformed the question of fraternity between Hindus and Muslims. With partition, for the first time, the brother acquired a distinctive sense of the 'foreigner' in the midst."[30]

These reports also mention a level of *leadership* that is missing earlier. The Hindus who are named in the report "led a group of around 40 other persons." This is very different from the mobs that range between "100–2,000." All five Muslim complainants are also eyewitnesses who identify the accused before fleeing to a nearby relief camp. They *see* the accused burning their houses, vehicles, and garage. By mentioning the name, residence, and weapons carried by the accused, these reports break with the general pattern of anonymity that characterizes most reports.

By allocating agency to neighbors, these reports are reminders that no archive, however intent in reproducing the colonial template of timeless ethnic violence, is absolute. No single logic—not even erasure and repression—can close off the possibility of the trace that reveals another side to the archive. These reports support extensively documented facts about the 2002 violence: the organization and mobilization of violence by neighbors against neighbors. To be clear, simply naming individuals in a police report does not guarantee prosecution. In fact, the men mentioned in these last reports were charge-sheeted, but all of them were acquitted in 2005. From the perspective of legal outcome, the trace does not constitute a counter-archive. They are nevertheless a trace of the intimate form of antiminority violence in India. They may be too few to constitute a pattern, but regardless they mark an interruption.

In his deconstruction of the opposition between absence and presence, Jacques Derrida used the concept of the trace as a "mark of the absence of a presence, an always-already absent present."[31] Even though in everyday language, the trace is usually understood as a remainder of something that is left behind, the concept refers to the differences, deferral, and displacement that is inherent in discourses that pretend to stand for unity, closure, and structure. The trace is a ripple within the archive, a mere five reports in an archive of over one hundred, and yet it opens the potential for composing the archive outside its own terms—not majorities versus minorities, Hindus versus Muslims, mobs versus mobs, but the terror of not being able to distinguish between neighbor and enemy.

"Just Another Piece of Paper"

2.1
Police and legal records lying on top of an almirah in the JF office.

In my last visit to the JF office, I noticed huge bundles covered in old sheets lining the stairs that lead from the office to the terrace. They looked like bags of laundry. They were full of legal applications, police reports, photocopies of judgments, and binders full of case papers—JF had painstakingly built this archive over the last decade. Covered in dust, it was now ready to be sold as scrap. Five years ago, these papers were stored in brand new shiny steel cabinets under lock and key and were often at the center of disputes between paralegals and lawyers, who blamed each other for misplacing and manhandling the papers. Now they were abandoned in the verandah, yellowing in the sun, splashed with pigeon shit, exposed to the rain. When I saw the papers decomposing in the terrace and the balconies of the JF office, the words of the *Times of India* report that opened this chapter returned to me as prophecy: "Just another piece of paper."

At one time these documents were at the origin of the dream of exposing the state and the first step toward justice; now they were lying in heaps, strewn about with broken dishes, chairs, and empty packets of tobacco. What reduced legal and police documents to "just another piece of paper" was more than the cunning of the state. Regardless of all the painstaking work that JF put into acquiring, filing, and storing these papers, they were caught in a paradox that touches all archives—how to compose them beyond the constraints with which they were created. No doubt activists had skillfully deployed progressive legislation like the RTI Act to force the Gujarat police to reveal much more than it wanted to. Even though they were aware of the extensive manipulation of evidence by the Gujarat police, JF nevertheless held onto the fantasy of the archive to expose state wrongdoing. But when trying to correct and amend FIRs, lawyers and paralegals realized that the problem with archives is not simply that they are inaccessible or secret or false but that they are constituted by forms that are hard to undo and repurpose for new ends.

Archives of violence can be characterized by what Derrida called an "archive of the destruction of the archive."[32] Derrida used this paradoxical formulation to talk about the South African Truth and Reconciliation commission and its attempt to archive apartheid. If one problem with archives of violence is that they often destroy the very thing they are supposed to archive, the other major problem is that by looking at police archives, we see through the eyes of the State. The archive was a place from where one could challenge power (activists forced Gujarat police to archive violence by registering FIRs), but it was also simultaneously the place where power manifested itself (the Gujarat police manipulated and erased the violence at the very moment of archiving it).

At one level, the police archive blurred the boundary between archives of violence and the violence of archives. As activists and lawyers accumulated documents, they opened the possibility of memorializing, recovering, and even challenging state accounts of violence. And yet the archive JF assembled fundamentally masked, misrepresented, and erased the violence they wanted to expose to the law. These two contradictory properties of the archive are inherent in the concept of the archive itself—no archive can preserve everything or indeed destroy everything.[33]

I have focused on composing the archive through minor *forms* to give a sense of the relationship between forms of reporting violence and its relationship with scenes of antiminority violence. Archives of violence do not simply erase or repress violence; they also repeat, temporalize, and aggregate it in ways that produce a specific relationship between majorities and minorities. Recent scholarship on documents and archives has focused on the materiality, circulation, and interpretation of documents in the formation of the modern state. In particular, scholars have focused on the powerful constitutive effects of documentation that can "produce the very persons and societies that ostensibly use them."[34] For instance, colonial records in India were "bound up with technologies of governing" insofar as the colonial state's obsession with writing reports and records reflected its practice of "rule-by-records."[35] The underlying assumption of such record-keeping was "that society could be represented as a series of facts, that the form of these facts was self-evident, and that administrative power stemmed from an accurate knowledge and an efficient use of the facts."[36] The exposure model similarly approaches the archive as a storehouse of facts and figures that can be wrested away from the control of the state to expose it. But this approach is not without its own perils, especially when "illegibility and opacity have been produced by the very instruments of legibility."[37] Archives also exercise their power by keeping things on the surface, repeating them, leaving things blank, and aggregating them.

Against the Witness

IN 2008, MAQBOOLBHAI, a trustee on the board of Idgah mosque in Mad-havnagar, showed me the place where the boy was shot. We were standing in the middle of a busy traffic intersection, and all that remained of the spot where the boy fell was a small patch of wild grass. A Hindu mob, which comprised local shopkeepers, had dragged him to the mosque that was later burned down, pulled down his pajamas to check if he was a Muslim, and then bludgeoned him with sticks and stones. The local police inspector had then walked over and shot the boy. Across the street, Maqboolbhai and other Muslims watched the killing. Outnumbered, they were scared to cross the street and recover the corpse. Maqboolbhai pointed to the patch of grass where the mob had abandoned the body. "He rotted on the street like a dog, the sun beating down, the crows pecking at his corpse. Only after a few days, when it was safe to cross the street, we brought him back."

The pronoun *we* suggests that he wasn't alone. Like Muslims across Gujarat who saw their neighbors loot, burn, and kill on the street, the witness was rarely ever alone at the scene. Another neighbor, Abdul, had a grocery and dairy shop that was burned down by Hindu mobs in 2002 and then again in 2011. Abdul agreed to work with Justice First (JF), a legal aid NGO, to testify against the accused in the courtroom. I first met seventy-four-year-old Abdul, a pious and soft-spoken man who was always dressed in crisp and spotless white kurta pajama, in his shop. He had joined JF in 2006 as a "consent-witness," which meant he received free legal services associated with his 2002-related case if he agreed to testify against the accused. After eight years, his case had reached the deposition stage and he was getting ready to testify before the judge. Bharat and Yasim, the JF paralegal and lawyer in charge of his case, had reached Abdul's shop for a final meeting. The advocate-paralegal team had been in touch with him since 2006. Finally, the moment had come when, as the JF lawyer put it, "the witness is on his own."

When we reached his shop, Yasim pulled out a thin folder with Abdul's case papers wedged between the handlebars of his motorbike. The shop was bustling with customers, and he waited for a free moment. Yasim leaned across the counter with the file open in one hand and began speaking in a low voice. The shop was on a busy street, and the sound of traffic was so loud that Yasim had to lean across the counter:

YASIM: Do you remember your statement? Your deposition is at 11 a.m. tomorrow.

ABDUL: [Handing out bags of milk to customers] I went to... they came to burn my shop... I recognize them and their names are...

YASIM: Yes... but you forgot to mention the name of X and Y...

ABDUL: These boys have grown up in front of me. I see them walking on the street in the evenings. I recognize all of them...

Abdul's shop was one of only three Muslim shops in the lane. It was doing good business. A steady stream of customers bought sodas and small pouches of tobacco. No one seemed to notice Yasim's file and his questions. When they finished, I asked Abdul a few questions.

M: So is everything all right?

ABDUL: Yes, sorry, I would chat with you... but right now I don't have my son to help me. He has left for the evening prayers.... I recognize all of them [the accused] and for that matter, even their fathers. They have grown up in this neighborhood.

M: This happened eight years ago, do you face any problems because of going to court? Has anybody apologized?

ABDUL: No one has apologized. They [the accused] send their friends and acquaintances to my shop.... To say they've been falsely accused... and they were not part of the mob that burned my shop...

M: So?

ABDUL: I told them, listen, I know these boys and I must go to court.

Abdul's calm confidence was striking. And, accordingly, I prepared myself to see him identify the accused in the courtroom. I felt lucky to have caught this moment, something that was in the making for almost a decade. The next morning, I entered courtroom number 15 of the Civil and Sessions Court in Ahmedabad with a deep bow in the direction of the judge, as did all the lawyers who entered before me. I hoped that no one noticed as I entered and sat quietly at the back of the room. Bharat, who had been preparing Abdul for five years for this day, melted into the crowd outside the courtroom, for fear of being associated with the trial. In other cases, the defense had tried to weaken the prosecution's case by implying that NGOs and activists were behind the cases. He pretended to chat on his mobile phone like others milling about outside the room. The courtroom lacked any pomp and show; it was a large, poorly maintained room with five rows of wooden benches. The judge sat alone on a long raised desk, and on his left a clerk examined documents before placing them before him. He kept mumbling to his clerk. I strained to hear what he was saying, but it was impossible to make out the words.

On the left of the judge, Abdul stood inside the wooden witness box and was speaking in spurts. The only words booming in the courtroom were of one speaker alone, the defense lawyer, who was no ordinary lawyer. Mr. Shah was an Ahmedabad-based criminal lawyer, publicly affiliated with the far-right Hindu organization the World Hindu Council. In 2002, he came forward to help hundreds of Hindus accused procure bail. In 2003, the Gujarat government appointed him the chief public prosecutor at the Ahmedabad sessions court, where more than 950 riot-related cases came up for hearing. Shah was also famous for scaring witnesses, which included both what he said and how he said it. He was cross-examining Abdul, pacing the small space in front of the judge, gesticulating with his arms, pointing at Abdul and shouting:

DEFENSE LAWYER (DL): So how many Muslim shops are there in your lane?

ABDUL: There are only a few shops ... [inaudible]

DL: Is it true that your shop is in a Muslim area?

ABDUL: Yes, there are Muslims shops in my area and there are also Hindu shops...

DL: So why was only your shop attacked? I am sure there are business rivalries in the market, otherwise why would only your shop be attacked? Maybe rival Muslims with whom you had a prior enmity came and burned your shop.

ABDUL: That is not true.

The JF lawyer did not interrupt Mr. Shah. Abdul's cross-examination ended abruptly. After the end of the cross-examination, the judge spoke a few words, left from a door behind his chair, and then everyone exited the room. I followed Bharat, Yasim, and Abdul down the stairs to the canteen to get a cup of tea.

YASIM: What happened? Why didn't you identify the accused?

ABDUL: This was the first time I had entered a courtroom.... I was very scared to stand in the witness box. My heart was pounding when they read the names of the accused and asked me to identify them.

BHARAT: It's okay, don't worry, many people feel the same, it's the way he [defense lawyer] shouts at the witnesses.... He has scared other witnesses before this...

YASIM: Yes, but why did you say in court that the names in your police statement... you had heard from others?

ABDUL: Well, it's been eight years since I have seen the accused and they kept shuffling them before me. I also did not recognize the names by which they called them out.... I was afraid of sending someone innocent to jail.... My body started to shiver... in the dock... and I was not sure how the names and the faces matched. What if I made a mistake, they could say I am lying and send me to jail? The defense lawyer was saying that I am lying.... I have never entered a courtroom before...

Abdul did not identify the accused in court. Instead, he told the judge that he had "heard about them [the accused] from others." Abdul's hands trembled as he sipped his cup of tea. Yasim gulped down his tea and left in a huff. Now that Abdul was no longer an eyewitness, the prosecution declared him a hostile witness. This was my first experience of seeing the courtroom turn against the witness. It became clear over time that Muslims were subjected to violence that was both publicly approved and legally inadmissible. The *form* of the violence—the participation of the public, the proximity and involvement of the police in the attacks, the intimacy of neighbors attacking each other (insofar as the rioters were also often neighbors), and the segregation of space (Hindu and Muslim shops doing business beside each other but living in religiously segregated neighborhoods)—these characteristics of the violence were framed by the judge, police, and defense during the trial to make Muslims into unreliable and false witnesses. If the minority is an ongoing process of making a certain kind of subject and subjectivity, which is always more than a question of number, then what can we learn from criminal trials that dismantle the minority as witness?

There are many good reasons for Abdul whose shop was burned down by his Hindu neighbors twice in six years—2002 and 2011—to not identify the accused. He may have been threatened by them but unwilling to tell the paralegals about it; he may have decided to bury the issue in exchange for peace or money or both; he may have been told not to identify the accused by Muslim leaders in the neighborhood who I heard from others had dissuaded them from going to the courts; or as he told me in subsequent conversations, he may have wanted to identify only a few people he was sure about but got intimidated by the defense lawyer who suggested that he was making false accusations about his neighbors.

The crisis of witnessing experienced by Abdul when he entered the courtroom tells us something about the role played by trials in the minoritization of Muslims. To be a minority is not only to be exposed to pogroms and lynching and then watch your attackers roam the streets freely afterwards, but it is also the experience of a crisis of witnessing in the face of collective violence that is public, and well known, but legally dismissed. This is not the failure of the law to recognize violence, but the legal transformation of collective violence into a force that undoes the ground underneath the witness. If the police, lawyers, and judges both shape and advance "the structures of domination that prevail in the wider social order," in the unmaking of the witness we glimpse the *making* of this wider social order itself.[1] My point is that this wider social order is also the delineation of a minority.

In other words, the crisis of witnessing experienced by survivors like Abdul was a lesson in what it means to be a Muslim in Gujarat. For Muslims, to bear witness to the pogrom meant standing before the law as malicious witnesses, as subjects who could be forced to accuse themselves. This crisis of witnessing was procedural (using police documents and evidence collection), affective (using voice, body, and language during the cross-examination), and fundamentally born of the disjuncture between collective violence and individual testimony.

Crisis of Witnessing

Since political violence like pogroms and riots also constitute forms of belonging, they are not simply destructive acts conducted on a mass scale.[2] The tension between the legal reckoning of individual harm and the collective nature of ongoing violence against certain groups produces a crisis of witnessing that is also a mode of minoritization.

At one level, subalterns turning hostile in the courtroom is hardly surprising. It can be understood as a standard aspect of the criminal legal system insofar as courts often support state power and can promote victor's justice in the aftermath of mass violence.[3] Scholars of trials show that trials often silence victim's experiences. Pratiksha Baxi analyzes rape trials to show that the hostile witness plays a key role in making sexual violence a public secret.[4] Rape trials rather than unveiling the truth behind pervasive sexual violence against women become a way of "knowing what not to know."[5] Anthropologists of post-conflict trials have shown that legal testimony often excludes and represses survivors' experiences.[6]

While anthropologists have focused on the politics of testimony, including erasures in the production and performance of legal testimony, literary scholars and philosophers have framed the difficulties of testimony in the face of extreme violence to understand the "unspeakable" and "impossible" aspects of language and the world itself. Approaching witnessing from the context of the Holocaust, Shoshana Felman and Dori Laub have argued that the Holocaust was "an event without a witness"—an event that eliminated its own witness.[7] The Holocaust was an event "whose literally *overwhelming evidence* makes it, paradoxically, into an *utterly proofless event*."[8] Their work pushes us to think about the impossibility of witnessing itself. What these two very different approaches to the "crisis of witnessing" share is an interest in using testimony to *expose* the limits of law, history, and politics to deal with extraordinary violence. Especially in more philosophical and literary approaches, the crisis of witnessing becomes a means to *expose* the trauma, experience, and politics that the law represses. This focus on the impossibility of witnessing leads scholars to turn to art and literature to reveal what cannot be said by the witness before the law. In this way, approaches to testimony, especially those that analyze its crisis in the face of limit cases, are embedded in what I have called the politics of exposure.

I suggest that the crisis of witnessing, seen through the perspective of trials in the aftermath of violence, gives an infrastructural dimension to the making of majorities and minorities. This is different from the exploration of testimony as a mode of understanding the limits of human existence and expression. What I have in mind is the role of ordinary law in the making and maintenance of the minority-majority relationship.[9] What I found in domestic-level post-riot trials in Gujarat are legal proceedings that are part of a wider process of making Muslims a minority: trials that show individuals and communities their second-class status in a majoritarian society by making it dangerous if not impossible for them to speak against the majority. This crisis of testimony is not epochal but infrastructural; it is not the magnitude of the event, the unspeakable trauma of past violence, the lack of a universal language, the blindness of the law, but a process of minority-making, a legal process that produces a section of the population that can see but not witness. This is not the erasure of victims' testimony, which is well known, but a process that builds on the disjuncture between social and legal witnessing to make the witness suspect, unreliable, and malicious.

To be clear, I am not interested here in unveiling the real reason behind Abdul's decision to not testify against the accused. Instead of asking "what really happened," I ask what was produced by what happened and what did activists, lawyers, and judges do with what happened? For instance, how did JF react? This was obviously a setback to the prosecution's case in the conventional legal sense. It weakened their case. As the number of Muslims turning hostile in the court increased, JF lawyers avoided any discussion of such cases with me. They were guarded, even hostile at times, about having me attend trials, but they were especially averse to discussing cases where people they had been working with for years refused to identify the accused. The lawyers were quick to blame paralegals for not giving witnesses adequate psychological support. The lawyers argued that the witnesses were too weak to withstand the pressure of cross-examination and once they entered the "witness box" they lost control of them. What was unspoken or rarely mentioned was an underlying suspicion that the witness had compromised with the accused in exchange for safety, land, or money without informing JF, which would make sense because JF was ethically against such out-of-court settlements. When I met Abdul a week later, he was deeply apologetic:

ABDUL: I feel terrible about what happened that day.... Yasim [lawyer] and Bharat [paralegal] put in a lot of hard work... they have been coming here for so many years...

M: I came here to talk to you about what you felt that day.... I hope you're feeling better now...

ABDUL: I am much better now...

M: So, what happened that day?

ABDUL: I'll be honest with you—I did not see the accused with my own eyes. Some of us [Muslim shop owners] fled, but others managed to see the perpetrators and gave us their names later. We decided to register our complaint with the police accordingly.

M: But you said that you knew them [the accused] very well... you knew them when they were children...

ABDUL: The judge announced names that I did not recognize.... And when they called the accused out, they kept shuffling them about and called them by names that I did not recognize.... I was scared to put names to faces, what if I made a mistake? The judge may have accused me of lying.... In a mob, how can I say the exact number of persons, there could be more or less...? I just wanted to name a few...

Abdul's response shows the effects of picking out an individual witness to describe political violence against an entire community. He mentioned he had felt afraid in the dock since it was his first time in a courtroom but in the same breath also said that he could not recognize their names. That is, he did not "recognize" the names that were uttered in the courtroom. But he also said that he had not seen the perpetrators with *his own eyes* (he elaborated that it was because of the distance and his poor eyesight) but heard their names from fellow Muslim shopkeepers. What matters is that he was a witness of a collective attack on Muslims, and it was this collective nature of the attack that was precisely inadmissible in the courtroom. Activists and paralegals who were keenly aware of the collective attack on Muslims could not undo this structure of legal witnessing in the courtroom.[10]

To avoid confronting the truth that the law was itself a mode of minoritization, lawyers preferred to consider each case psychologically. They described Abdul's weaknesses as a witness—his old age, his frail health, and his meek temperament. What was at stake here were structural questions about the inadequacy of trials to address the intimacy between the witness and the accused, the limits of individual testimony, and the defense's use of rituals of humiliation and rites of domination in the courtroom.[11] These questions were never asked or debated in meetings because they pointed to the limits of legal exposure and its imagination of the heroic witness speaking truth to power.

"In Front of Our Eyes"

The poet Cathy Park Hong describes the feeling of being "robbed of one's eyes" when police murders of Black men in the United States, witnessed by dozens of witnesses and recorded on cell phones, end up in acquittals.[12] She writes that "witness accounts matter little when prosecutors can mishandle evidence and mislead the jury; when evidence is up against the Law that makes impossible the criminal conviction of police officers who act with impunity."[13] Being robbed of one's eyes is part of the affective dimension of being a minority. To be a minority means to be repeatedly robbed of one's eyes, not simply as individuals but as members of a group who are both individually and collectively disbelieved. The criminal legal system's focus on individual culpability was repurposed by the Gujarat state to make Muslims untrustworthy and malicious witnesses during the trial. A good place to understand how this process began is to read Abdul's original police complaint:

> Due to the communal incident [*quomi banavana*] in Godhra on 27.02.2002, the VHP (World Hindu Council) announced a "Gujarat Bandh" (shutdown) on 28.02.2002, but I still opened my milk shop for business but suddenly in the afternoon communal violence [*quomi toofan*] broke out in X, Y and Z areas of the city and then *all the shopkeepers* in my line of shops closed their shop and fled toward the mill. In front of *our eyes*, mobs of several thousand damaged and burned shops, vehicles, cabins, and houses.
>
> The communal mob [*quomi tola*] that destroyed and burned the shops *belonging to the Muslim community*, including my shop, comprised 1) A alias B, 2) C, 3) D alias E, 4) F, 5) his brother G alias H, 6) I, 7) J alias K, 8) L, 9) M's brother, 10) N, 11) O and thousands of others were present

in the mob. The above named persons in the communal mob were seen setting fire to the shops. Due to the destruction, my shop suffered losses of 100,000 rupees. (emphasis mine)

Notice that the report begins in the first person singular but shifts to the plural as soon as the violence starts. Recall here this report's similarity with the collective witnessing of the murder of a Muslim boy that opens this chapter. Even though the First Information Report is signed by Abdul as an individual, it is written in the collective: it uses "our" and "we" instead of the singular "I." This is true not only for Abdul's report but all the four eyewitness reports. Together, then, the report describes a *collective* witnessing of a *public* attack on Muslim shops. A key part of Abdul's struggle in the courtroom is to articulate this collective attack and its community witnessing in the face of a trial that isolates him.

Within the adversarial format of the trial, the legal process stages a debate between two different interpretations of the violence, which is more than simply the erasure of violence against minorities. What is at stake here are the limits of minority witnessing and what happens to Muslims when they accuse Hindus of attacking them. For the prosecution, the violence was an "attack on Muslim shops" and that the "accused gathered illegally with the common motive [*eraado*] to destroy and burn Muslim property." This common motive is not only dismissed by the judge but, by the end of the trial, the Hindu mob is transformed into a crowd of noncriminal bystanders. In turn, Muslims become false accusers. The defense lawyers alleged that the police inspector in charge of the case was also working under Muslim pressure. Here is what the police inspector says in court responding to the defense's allegation in his cross-examination:

It is not true that I [police sub-inspector] have filed this complaint under the pressure of Muslim leaders [*agaevano*]. It is not true that this complaint was written in the presence of Muslim leaders. It is not true that I have written this complaint to comply with Muslim leaders.

Regardless of the veracity of these allegations, what is important to note here is the construction of the Muslim witness as a sign of a Muslim conspiracy against Hindus. This becomes clearer when we consider Gafar, the second eyewitness in the case. Gafar, a Muslim mechanic, was twenty-four when he saw his garage and home burned down along with Abdul's. He was the second JF-supported eyewitness in the case and, unlike Abdul, moved out of Madhavnagar to live and work in a Muslim-majority area of the city. The fact that he no longer lived in Madhavnagar perhaps played an important role in his ability to identify the accused in the courtroom, and yet he too had difficulty recognizing them. He deposed in court a month before Abdul on August 16, 2010.

On the afternoon of February 28, 2002, a mob attacked Gafar's garage. He fled toward the nearby mill (like Abdul). He named seven people in his FIR and went on to identify four in the courtroom. Three of them had aliases—"A person H *dada* [a suffix added to the name to communicate a "strong man"], and a person whose name I don't know but I can identify him when I see him." One of the men he identified by an alias was then asked his name by the judge. When the accused gave a different name, not his alias, to the judge, Gafar responded, "The accused says his names is D but we recognized him as H."

What is the status of this "we"? If one aspect of the "we" is the Muslim community and shopkeepers in the neighborhood, then the second aspect of the "we" is the intimacy between victims and perpetrators. As I discuss in chapter 1, some of the accused are well-known criminals in the area, known to Muslims by their aliases but not their formal names. During his cross-examination, Gafar admits, "I do not know the proper name of Hanuman." Out of the eleven accused mentioned by all the four eyewitnesses in the case, *four have aliases*, and one is identified only by his brother's name. Here, the difference between aliases and formal names is a technicality used to dismiss Gafar's testimony but on closer examination, it is another instance of the social relationships of intimacy and proximity embedded in anti-Muslim attacks that is inadmissible in the courtroom.

Abdul's reversal in the courtroom and Gafar's failure to identify the accused with their formal names was construed by JF as a failure. And yet this is not merely individual or psychological failure but a failure produced through practices like the way police arranged accused in the courtroom, the defense lawyer's tenor of cross-examination, and the structural limitations of individual testimony in the aftermath of a pogrom.

The Place of Witnessing

To be a minority means that the place of witnessing, both literally as the site of violence and figuratively as the standpoint from where the witness speaks, comes undone in the courtroom. Over the course of the trial, the place of the Muslim witness becomes untenable through both displacement and emplacement. As the trial proceeded, the chasm between Abdul and Gafar's world and the world of the law kept on expanding. By the end of the trial, they became unreliable witnesses who had been contradicted by police documents, their own previous statements to the police, the nature of the violence, and finally by the very fact of having survived the violence.

After Gafar identified the accused in court, the defense during cross-examination asked him to prove that he was at the site of violence. Gafar claimed that he lived inside the garage that was burned down. In response, the defense lawyer alleged that Gafar could not have seen the accused because he did not live in his garage. He questioned Gafar's status as an eye-witness by asking him to provide official documentation such as electricity bills or property tax receipts to prove that he did indeed live in or even own the shop. Here is what Gafar says in court:

> I [Gafar] have lived inside my shop for five years before the incident. I have no documents, or a ration card to prove that during the incident I used to live in the shop. I have no documents to prove that I was the owner of my shop. This shop belonged to my father. I have no documents to prove that this shop belonged to my father.

Earlier, the defense used the formal, on paper, name of the accused to rob the witness of his eyes, and in this instance the very ground on which the witness stands is taken away from him for lack of paperwork. If at one level this seems more evidence for the law's fondness to believe the written, and only "what itself has written,"[14] there is more to this than the use of technicalities by shrewd lawyers to win their cases. The lawyers are eager not only to rob the witness of his eyes but to cast him as a permanent outsider, a Muslim.

To present Gafar as an outsider, the defense lawyer asks him if it is better for him to give answers in Hindi (rather than the local language, Gujarati). To pose this question is to make him appear as a non-Gujarati. When he responds that he can answer in both languages, the defense lawyer points out that his police statement was in fact in Hindi. Later the judgment repeats this remark as part of a long list of revelations that emerged during Gafar's cross-examination. If on the one hand, the trial tries to displace Gafar from the site of violence, then at the same time, it tries to place him squarely within a communal space. Thus, one long section of Gafar's cross-examination simply puts "on record" that the violence took place in a Muslim neighborhood. Here is an excerpt from that section:

It is true that on one side of the bridge there is New Manek chowk mill and on the other side there is a Muslim settlement [*muslim vasahat*]. It is true that there is a mosque where Asarwa bridge meets Idgah circle. It is true that on one side of the Idgah circle there is the Idgah police station. It is true that on Idgah circle the corporation has made a big roundabout and Muslims have settled around it...

This description of the religious composition of the site of violence may seem innocuous, but it is one more step in the making of a world made up of Hindus and Muslims, separate and at war with each other. At one point, Abdul has to tell the court, "It is true that the area where I live and work is a Muslim area." According to the defense's argument, *both* Hindus and Muslims were rioting, and therefore it is either impossible to identify the accused or both are equally liable. Indeed, these acts of putting witnesses "in their place" means that the defense can suggest that Muslims may have destroyed Abdul's shop out of enmity.

"For eight days I stayed at the site of violence but no Hindu killed me." Gafar makes this statement during his cross-examination when asked if anyone attacked him after his shop was burned down. This is only one question among others that puts him in a position where he must choose between the status of a survivor or a witness. Both Abdul and Gafar's shops were close to the Idgah police station [*chowki*], which did not prevent them from being destroyed, but this proximity to the police, just like their proximity to Hindu shops, was used in the cross-examination to undermine their testimony.

"It is true that there is police station across the road, but I did not register any complaint ... for 8 days I stayed near the site of the incident but I did not go to the police station to file a complaint regarding the incident. During those eight days I did not go to the police station."

No one asked Gafar why he didn't go to the police station. We find an explanation in the original complaint given to the police by another witness who retracted his statements during the trial. "The city was very unsafe after the event, and curfew was declared, and because there was no security of life, I did not file a complaint till today, there is no other reason." If we step outside the courtroom, there is no dearth of reports mentioning that Gujarat police were aiding the rioters in many areas of Ahmedabad, and many Muslims died because of police firing, not riotous mobs. In the Human Rights Watch report on Gujarat 2002, titled after the police remark made during the pogrom, "We Have No Orders to Save You," survivors describe how the police refused to register their complaints, attacked them, and tried to implicate them in the cases as rioters.

Two months after the riots, the National Human Rights Commission of India (NHRC) found that "the victims of atrocities were facing great difficulty in having FIRs recorded, in naming those whom they identified and in securing copies of their FIRs."[15] A *Hindustan Times* report from February 20, 2012, based on the Gujarat government's official statistics of deaths in police firing, shows that the police killed more Muslims than Hindus. The Concerned Citizens Tribunal reported that "not only did the police not do anything to stop Hindu mobs . . . they actually turned their guns on the helpless Muslim victims."[16] The People's Union for Democratic Rights (PUDR) report describing the role of the police in the anti-Muslim riots said, "During the course of the carnage the role of the police, or rather, its absence has been most noticeable. It was so conspicuous because the police were one actor during the carnage which departed significantly and consistently from its assigned role."[17] None of this public knowledge about the police's involvement in the pogrom is considered during the trial, and the judge simply writes that the witness filed a complaint with the police only "24–25 days *after the event* and there is no explanation for this delay."

We can read the trial as a tool to erase state violence against Muslims, but such a reading will not help us understand a key outcome of these trials: the way they transform public violence against Muslims to produce them as outsiders, to separate them from the majority. I mean how defense lawyers and public prosecutors and judges adapt the standard features of criminal law in India to disbelieve Muslims who witness, and have survived, state-sanctioned public violence. No doubt many features of what I am describing here are precisely how defense lawyers secure acquittals in routine criminal cases across India, but what is different in the case of Gujarat is both the scale and nature of the violence and what is produced by the legal encounter: *a subject who can either survive the violence or witness it.* To repeat, the trial does not simply overlook the violence that comes up for examination, nor does it merely flatten it, but it produces a subject who is dismissed because he has survived. In the words of the judgment: "One more matter to note is that there is mention [*sic*] of a mob of 3–4000 people stoning each other and that this stoning continued for half an hour and the witness fled to the mill to save his life at this time, therefore it is not possible to maintain that the witness could at that time recognize and identify the accused."[18]

These comments remind us of Agamben's proposition about the "impossible dialectic" between the untrustworthy witness (the survivor) and the genuine witness (who is dead), but with a key difference.[19] In the crisis faced by Muslim witnesses, we get a sense not so much of an ontological split, the limits of language itself, but the creation of a subject who stands before the law as a minority—a sectarian and false witness.

Recomposing Witnessing

Abdul and Gafar experienced in the courtroom an unmaking, a displacement, not simply from their home during the violence but from the space of legal witnessing; the world as they knew and experienced it was dismissed by the law. If I had to distill this crisis of witnessing into a sentence, it would be a phrase that I often heard in the courtroom and saw in court transcripts: *We saw them with our eyes. I am no longer in a position to recognize them.* As the collective "we" outside the courtroom became an individual "I" inside it, the witness became undone. That all this happened without fanfare in the lower courts of Ahmedabad means that the exhortation to "bear witness" in the aftermath of political violence does not address the wider issue of the minoritization of Muslims in India.

Before I close, I want to give a glimpse of an effort by activists to compose witnessing differently. A public event that attempted to address the ongoing minoritization of Muslims in Gujarat. In February 2011, I attended an event organized by two NGOs, ANHAD (Act Now for Harmony and Democracy) and the Center for Social Justice, to commemorate nine years of the pogrom. The invitation was sent to the JF office in the form of a small black postcard-sized card that announced in bold lettering, "PUBLIC HEARING: Exposing the Unseen: Tracing the Lies of Muslims in Gujarat post-2002." Along with the time and venue, it mentioned the eminent "jury" who would hear the witnesses: a retired judge, a writer, the founder of a local NGO, and a member of the National Commission for Minorities. As the language of a "hearing" and a "jury" suggest, the event did not disavow the power of the legal model. The organizers repurposed the legal setup—a jury, testimony, and a judgment—as a frame for the witnesses to convey the ongoing minoritization of Muslims in all areas of life in Gujarat. The witnesses—not just Muslims, and not only victims of violence—described discrimination in infrastructure and housing, lack of educational facilities and scholarship, and the prolonged detention, harassment, and torture of Muslim men after they were labeled as "terrorists." Activists used PowerPoint presentations to describe the plight of Muslim survivors of the pogrom, permanently displaced from their homes, now living in "relief colonies" without potable drinking water, sewage, regular electricity, or essential institutions like schools and transport.

Let me describe the first witness, an elderly man dressed in spotless white kurta pajama and a white prayer cap. He was the father of a young Muslim man who was in jail on charges of terrorism. The father of the terror accused, he was asked to sign blank pages or face endless detention in the police station. He was made to wait in a police station for six days. The police officer relented only when he signed those blank papers. The father asked the jury and the audience, "imagine if they did this to me, what would they have done with those innocent children who the police have framed as terrorists." In this public hearing, the father of a terror accused could speak freely because it was no longer simply about an exceptional and single event, but the structural, systematic, and official discrimination of Muslims both within and beyond the law. This is not simply a difference between individual and collective victimhood. It is the difference between the isolation of the witness in the courtroom versus the collective experience of becoming a minority.

Take the example of another speaker, an academic whose house was attacked in 2002: Professor J. S. Bandukwalla began his speech by announcing that the chief minister was fully involved with "whatever happened" in Gujarat. Not only was the pogrom political, the professor went on to argue that many within the Muslim community were collaborating with the current Hindu supremacist regime. He spoke about a range of topics affecting Muslims—ghettoization, lack of scholarships, and public infrastructure—and he ended his words with a plea that "we want to live like full-fledged first-rate citizens...no one should be able to say that you [Muslim] are a second-class citizen." In his remarks on some sections of the Muslim community, the wealthier Dawoodi Bohras, who had joined the current regime, the professor used caste and class differences among Muslims to fracture the idea of Muslims as a homogenous category.

As an example of an activist effort to compose testimony outside legal exposure, the public hearing moved in the opposite direction of the legal trial; the trial isolated the witness, cross-examined him to destabilize the ground on which he was standing. The public hearing brought together a diverse set of actors, not all of whom were Muslims or survivors of the pogrom, who spoke from their different locations as witnesses and activists about a collective process of minority-formation. Unlike the trial that examined an event that was in the past, the public hearing addressed the experience of being a Muslim in the present, whether it was as a terror accused or a community activist.[20] To be clear, the public hearing did lean on the legal model of witnessing, and I am not suggesting that it was the perfect space to articulate the truth of being a Muslim in Gujarat. Rather, it was an attempt to use the legal as one of several elements that could be used to produce a space for witnessing not only what had happened but that which was happening. Only by composing disparate elements like arbitrary and illegal detention, the targeting of Muslims on charges of terrorism, police torture, the lack of scholarships and ration cards and the basic infrastructure like drinking water and sewage inside Muslim neighborhoods could the crisis of witnessing be transformed into something else, not heroic testimony, but a collective description of the role of the state in making Muslims into a permanent minority.

Anti-Impunity Activism

EVERY MORNING, I joined Bharatbhai, a Justice First (JF) paralegal in Ahmedabad, on his field visits to the homes of Muslim witnesses who were coming up for deposition. Sitting pillion on his motorbike, I carried his folders with copies of police statements, FIRs, and miscellaneous case papers. After chatting and sharing a cup of tea with witnesses, Bharatbhai would tell them important court dates. He would ask if they had received any summons from the court or faced any threats or intimidation from the accused. After these preliminaries, he would sit with their official statement in his hand and proceed to quiz the witness on his or her statement. The main thing to remember, he told them, are the four facts: date, time, name, and role of the accused.

> Perhaps these laws that we are trying to unravel they don't exist at all.
> —Kafka, *The Problem of Our Laws*

> So many like you come and record our stories, but nothing happens. So why should we make enemies for nothing?
> —Saiza Bano

To help them remember these facts, witnesses were given a typed copy of their statement and asked to memorize it in their spare time. They were expressly instructed not to add any content or interpretation to their "original" statements, answer to the point, and only repeat what was already "on record." To speak the truth in front of the judge and the legal process would take care of the rest. The paralegals had picked up this technique from the lawyers. This focus on facts and repetition helped JF reduce testifying in the courtroom into a simple matter of repetition. Testimony should include only four facts. Such ostensibly basic instructions were designed to make depositions easy for people who had never entered a courtroom before. But it also served another purpose: it made the struggle for justice entirely procedural. Difficult matters related to the intimate relationship between Muslim witnesses and the Hindu accused, the intimidation faced by Muslims in the courtroom, and the role of police documents on casting suspicion on the witness even before they had entered the courtroom were cast outside the framework of justice. This procedural adherence to rule of law ideology helped lawyers cut themselves off from all the messy aspects of cases that were not simply criminal but also fundamentally political.[1] And yet everyone knew that much more than the basic facts of the case were at stake in 2002-related trials.

In May 2011, the final arguments of a case concluded. The case had been dragging on because the Hindu accused didn't show up in court. Mehr, the JF lawyer working on the case, remained hopeful. She told me that the judge is "strict"—when some accused did not appear for several months and their lawyers kept making excuses for their absence, the judge scolded the police: "Bring the accused next month. Otherwise, I will pass non-bailable warrants against each of them." Soon, all the accused surfaced, their statements were recorded, the witnesses cross-examined, and the final arguments submitted. But when it was time for the court to pronounce its final judgment, local elections were going on. Narendra Modi, who was the chief minister during the violence in 2002 and had never lost an election, was running for his third term. When Mehr approached the judge for a speedy judgment, he told her privately, "It is best if I adjourn till the elections are over." The judge's comment showed that pogrom-related cases, unlike ordinary criminal cases, were entangled in the political rise of Hindu nationalism in Gujarat. It was clear that these trials were not isolated cases of criminality by individual miscreants, and yet it was precisely this framing of the violence that was the foundation of anti-impunity activism.

In another case, four out thirty-six Muslim witnesses were willing to settle the case outside the court if the Hindu accused rebuilt the wall of the cemetery that they had broken in 2002. But "compromise" was construed within JF as a failure to convict the accused, and both paralegals and lawyers were not comfortable discussing cases in which witnesses had retracted their statements in court. These often secretive out-of-court arrangements between the accused and witnesses were called *compro* (short for compromise) by the lawyers and paralegals and were a matter of embarrassment and shame since the whole point of going to the court was to secure a conviction. By 2010, the topic of compromise was even more alarming because they were showing up across districts, sometimes, unbeknownst to paralegals and lawyers.

In one legal meeting, the coordinator reported that in over half of the cases, Muslim witnesses had compromised with the Hindu accused. What was happening? In the villages, compromise was often related to the livelihood of the witness. The reasons for Muslims refusing to identify the accused in the court multiplied as time passed: the accused's brother supplied water to the witness's field; the accused and the witness were neighbors and perforce saw each other a lot; the eyewitness got a job in the Hindu nationalist party BJP's youth wing. The limitations of legal trials to address the entangled social lives of Hindus and Muslims meant that efforts for legal justice were reduced to correcting police statements, adding witnesses to cases, submitting records to the court, and documenting lapses in due process.

At one level, there is nothing exceptional about JF's struggle with criminal trials in the lower courts in India. It is well known that judicial delay and a staggering backlog of cases makes the Indian legal process a punishment for the poor and marginalized. And yet JF's effort to address impunity through the law takes on a different color and significance in the aftermath of state-sanctioned political violence against Muslims that is also the construction of a new kind of majority and minority. It points us to both the limits of law to address political violence against minorities and the paradoxical effects of legal exposure in contexts where people must live beside the people who have harmed them. Further, activist assumptions about the autonomy of the rule of law led to a form of procedural activism that was unable to respond to the minoritization of Muslims both inside and outside the courtroom. The irony here is that not only did procedural activism fail to help Muslims secure justice, but it became a part of a legal process that further disempowered them and reinforced Hindu supremacy. The legal trials were used to assert the power of the Gujarat state to diminish and humiliate the witness.

What are the limits of anti-impunity activism in contexts of state-sanctioned public violence? What is the relationship between NGO activism and the wider process of minoritization? To answer these questions, I track the effects of seeking legal exposure for political violence that constitutes majority and minority populations. However, I don't stand *above* the activists, lawyers, and paralegals I worked with to pronounce judgment on their work as much as I hope to show the challenges of using the law to address violence against Muslims as I saw it from a place beside them.

These challenges arise from anti-impunity and human rights activists' focus on the punishment and prosecution of individuals through the rule of law and "due process"—a set of legal rules, rituals, and procedures—that can ostensibly be isolated from the social, cultural, and political context that produces antiminority violence. This assumption about the law had three effects. First, it turned the legal process on its head. The trials that were supposed to expose the violence against Muslims, instead exposed Muslims to legal violence—the structural forms of delay and deferral that marked the everyday life of a case in the lower courts in India. Second, turning to legal trials to combat impunity assumed that impunity—the power of mobs, state actors, and Hindu supremacists to attack Muslims and get away with it— was a force outside the law. This faith in the law as a magical tool and legality as an autonomous zone that existed outside the polarized social context in Gujarat did not account for the law as a semi-autonomous field that included within it heterogeneous elements like the illegal, the licit, and the legal.[2] It did not account for the simple fact that legal justice would perforce have to be performed through an infrastructure that was embedded in Hindu supremacy. Finally, in response to the impossibility of separating the rule of law from Hindu supremacy, human rights activists practiced a form of procedural activism that disregarded the entangled life of Hindus and Muslims in India.[3]

Justice First

Why did Muslims go to the court in the first place? JF's moral language of speaking truth to power and the efforts of its paralegals, who often belonged to the same neighborhood as the survivors and in some cases had suffered during the pogrom themselves, played a key role in persuading Muslims to go to the courts. Seeking justice from the courts was based on the underlying assumption (and fantasy) that the courtroom would be a space outside politics, outside the tentacles of Hindu supremacy, that suffused public culture and statecraft in Gujarat. The idea was that the legal process would become a space for persecuted Muslims to speak the language of rights and citizenship. By bringing hundreds of legal cases to trial, JF wanted to enter a zone outside the polarized social and political context—a context in which the

Hindu nationalist party had won every election in Gujarat since the pogrom, successfully dividing society into Hindus versus Muslims. This legal zone was assumed to be outside the present political conjuncture in Gujarat. Over the years, as Muslims entered the courtroom, they grew wary of this imagined legal space of citizenship and rights, and even JF paralegals and lawyers were no longer able to keep up the appearance that the law was outside the creation of Hindus as a permanent majority in Gujarat. The pogrom had passed, but it had produced a public and state-sanctioned Hindu supremacy that was unfolding in the present.

Describing the fetishism of legality in Africa, the Comaroffs write that the "law is attributed magical properties to achieve order, civility, justice and empowerment" in the face of widespread disorder because it is considered a neutral language to make claims on the state.[4] But this assumption of neutrality in matters concerning Muslims is precisely what was impossible in Gujarat. Hindu nationalists and the then chief minister Narendra Modi had cast anyone trying to draw attention to the violence against Muslims as anti-Gujarat and anti-Hindu.[5] JF paralegals and lawyers were only too aware of the partisan (anti-Muslim) nature of the state apparatus, including the bureaucracy and the police, and yet they persuaded Muslims to keep going to the court. This disassociation between the widespread exclusion of Muslims in social and political life and the assumptions about the neutrality of the law was reflected in JF's organization. The organization was split such that lawyers would be concerned with the trial—"the law"—and paralegals would address the "social"—helping survivors to come to court. But could one really ignore the fact that the witnesses were all Muslims? Or put in different terms, how could one separate the state that facilitated the attacks on Muslims from the state that was now supposed to punish individuals for participating in those attacks?

After a decade, it became difficult, even impossible, for paralegals like Bharatbhai to maintain the fiction that one day, in the end, the courts would punish Hindus. "How long can I convince them [Muslim survivors] to come to court when sometimes even the [JF] lawyer doesn't bother to show up and the witness end up losing a day's worth of wages," Bharatbhai told me one day while I helped him prepare Excel sheets on the computer: case history, court dates, and legal "action plan" in Hindi and English. Anti-impunity activism could not take on board the interconnected lives of the Hindu accused and Muslim witnesses. The passing of eight years between the event and the trial meant marriage, death, new livelihoods, and the sale and purchase of land between litigants. One JF lawyer working in the villages in the Anand district said, "It was becoming difficult to distinguish between victims and perpetrators. The [Muslim] victims tell the [Hindu] accused that our lawyers [Justice First] are pursuing the cases, not us!"

In 2004 the mood was different. Human rights activist and former member of the Indian Administrative Service Harsh Mander, along with the Lawyer's Collective, challenged the Gujarat police's decision to close thousands of pogrom-related cases before the Supreme Court of India. Based on their petition, the Supreme Court of India reopened nearly two thousand cases and ordered the establishment of a monitoring cell to review the closed cases. In the wake of this decision, hailed as a major victory for activists, JF began to train local Gujarati men and women as paralegals, who in turn would help Muslims to fight for justice in the courts. Since the paralegals were both Hindus and Muslims and included several individuals who had suffered losses during the pogrom, they were part of an attempt to launch a wider campaign for legal justice, peace, and reconciliation. JF leadership believed that by facilitating victims' access to the courts, Muslims would be able to access their rights guaranteed by the Constitution. Moreover, JF combined the moral language of Gandhian ethics (speak only the truth and offer no bribes) with standard elements of human rights discourse. They began their efforts by contacting as many affected Muslims as possible (and picking up over 250 cases) and offered to help them fight their case in the court for free if they wanted justice.

JF hired and trained twenty-five community justice workers across four districts, who in turn contacted Muslim survivors. They also hired and trained young local lawyers to monitor the progress of the cases in which paralegals had secured the complainant's consent. Once it collected information relating to all 2002-related police cases in Gujarat, its paralegals and lawyers approached hundreds of Muslim witnesses named in the police reports. They worked mostly with poor and self-employed Muslims— mechanics, shopkeepers, and laborers—who had no familiarity with court proceedings, and most had never entered a courtroom.

From the outset, there was a tension between the prosecutorial and the ethical. JF emphasized criminal prosecution and believed that even a majoritarian state apparatus could be used to hold itself accountable. At the same time, it also framed legal prosecution as a social movement for reconciliation. They tried to combine elements of both restorative (reconciliation) and retributive (punishment) justice but over time, courtroom procedural-ism trumped larger questions about inequality and poverty.[6]

Infusing Gandhian ideas of brotherhood and interreligious amity into anti-impunity discourse helped JF develop innovative strategies to gain the confidence of survivors and vernacularize the language of human rights. In practice, this meant that Hindus and Muslims were paired in one team and songs of universal brotherhood would often open meetings. All this was to set the noble intention among activists and lawyers to use only perfectly ethical techniques to achieve justice. And yet as the trials proceeded, the normative principles associated with the rule of law sat uneasily with the intimidation faced by Muslims and paralegals in the courtroom. JF's agenda, despite efforts to vernacularize rule of law ideology with Gandhian ideas, was aligned with global human rights activism and transitional justice efforts across world areas.[7] In other words, regardless of JF's well-intentioned efforts to vernacularize human rights to tackle impunity, insofar as the law worked within an individual victim/perpetrator model, anti-impunity could not account for the structure of power that had framed Muslims as a perma-nent minority.[8]

This brings us to the difference between domestic criminal courts and transitional justice mechanisms, especially because lawyers, activists, and judges in Gujarat were working within the limits of standard criminal law. The an-thropological critique of transitional justice mechanisms, especially the role of "the local" in understanding the impact of accountability, as well as the ways in which people respond to justice is helpful to understand the limits of anti-impunity efforts faced by JF in Gujarat.

Rosalind Shaw and Lars Waldorf argue that the local often destabilizes efforts for justice. They define the local as not merely a circumscribed level but "a standpoint based in a particular locality but not bounded by it."[9] In-sofar as such a standpoint must surely be the starting point to understand the nature of the violence itself, the local for my purposes is both the infra-structure of Indian legality, such as practices of proceduralism, delay, de-ferral, and police paperwork that undergird criminal law in India, and the state-sanctioned forms of intimate violence between Hindus and Muslims.[10] Muslims and Hindus were not simply victims and perpetrators, but also *neighbors*. It is this violent intimacy of the majority-minority relationship in India that constituted the limits of legal activism in Gujarat. Even though JF used constitutional language and Gandhian values like brotherhood to oppose Hindu supremacy, it assumed that the pogrom was an exceptional breakdown of the rule of law rather than explore the possibility that the law itself would become the space to perform Hindu supremacy. In this context, JF's recourse to the law ended up exposing Muslims to state spaces (the courtroom), procedures (cross-examination and documentation), and actors (police and judges) that reinforced the second-class status of Muslims in Gujarat.

Activists versus "the People"

As a response to the unprecedented international human rights and media attention on the Gujarat pogrom, the Hindu nationalist regime and the then chief minister of Gujarat, Narendra Modi, weaponized the question of accountability. They framed efforts to seek justice as an issue of insiders (the people of Gujarat) versus outsiders (activists and English media). This split was supported by the media response to the massacre, which itself was split along linguistic lines, with the vernacular media framing the attacks on Muslims as a spontaneous outburst of Hindu anger. The Hindu nationalist regime seized this split and projected the critique of the Gujarat government as an attack on "the people." Soon after the riots, Modi traveled across the state as part of a public campaign to protect *Gujaratni Asmita* (Gujarati Pride), describing activists and the political opposition as "outsiders" who were besmirching the good name of Gujarat and its people. Modi accused activists of "lending strength to anti-national elements" and "weakening the nation by undermining social values." Later, Hindu nationalists swept the elections by framing it as a referendum on the massacre, polarizing the electorate along religious lines.

When Hindu nationalists used the electoral victory as an expression of popular support that should effectively end all questions about accountability, activists and NGOs turned to the courts to expose the regime. Activists and lawyers filed petitions to open closed cases, transfer cases outside Gujarat, and expose state complicity in scuttling the investigation of Hindu nationalist politicians. In response, Chief Minister Modi labeled human rights workers as "five-star activists" [a reference to the alleged upper-class lifestyle of human rights activists pursuing justice in Gujarat] who were insulting the people of Gujarat. In September 2004, Human Rights Watch published a report that described the intimidation and harassment of witnesses, activists, and lawyers helping survivors to fight for accountability. It added that the state government has "consistently sought to impede successful prosecution of those allegedly involved in the massacres."[11] In 2015, Modi addressed the Indian judiciary in a public ceremony and said that they must not be swayed by "five-star activists" and continue to be fearless in their work. It had the desired effect. In 2022, the Supreme Court of India passed a judgment on a pogrom-related case that insinuated that human rights activists "kept the pot boiling, obviously, for ulterior design." The judges added that such persons "need to be in the dock and proceeded with in accordance with the law."[12] A day after the judgment, the Gujarat police arrested a high-profile activist.

In this context, where the state and the wider public had come together not once but twice (first during the pogrom and then by electing the Hindu nationalist regime to power) to assert Hindu supremacy, JF helped Muslim victims to approach the courts and gave them free legal services, proclaiming that the legal process is the ethical way for minorities to reclaim equal citizenship accorded to them by a secular constitution. In this, JF was part of a global trend often described as the judicialization of politics, where political battles for welfare, security, and transparency are being fought inside the courts.[13]

Activist and civil society faith in the courts, combined with the availability of special legal instruments like Public Interest Litigation, have thrust political questions of belonging and citizenship on Indian courts. This has produced what Erica Bornstein and Aradhana Sharma call "technomoral politics," which combines legal and moral languages and judicial activism.[14] JF's anti-impunity activism also combined moral and legal languages. But it was their imagination of the law as a weapon to expose the state that implicated their activism with everyday legality. By everyday legality, I mean the blurred boundaries between the legal and the illegal, the strategic manipulation of documentation and procedures by the legal bureaucracy, the opacity and arbitrariness that mark the everyday workings of lower courts, and the structural limitations of the adversarial legal system. It is well documented that these aspects of the criminal legal system routinely sanctify patriarchal and caste-based hierarchies in Indian society.[15]

The notorious "Best Bakery" case illustrates well the dangers of trying to combat Hindu supremacy through legal trials. The brief details of the case are as follows. A Hindu mob killed and burned fourteen Muslims inside a small bakery in Baroda in 2002. Of the fourteen, nine belonged to one family, and a nineteen-year-old girl, Zahira Sheikh, identified the accused who killed her family members. But during the trial in 2003, Zahira and her mother and brother, along with thirty-seven other key witnesses turned "hostile" (retracted their pre-trial statements in favor of the accused). A Hindu nationalist leader accompanied the prosecution's "star witness" Zahira to the court. Predictably, she told the judge that she saw nothing during the incident. Of the 120 witnesses, a third never testified, and of those who testified, more than half retracted their statements during the trial. In one of the first decisions taken by a "fast-track" court set up by the Gujarat government to deal with legal cases in the aftermath of the pogrom, the judge acquitted all twenty-one accused.

Later, Zahira appeared at a press conference organized by an NGO and said she had been intimidated and retracted her statement fearing the safety of her family. An investigative magazine carried a front-page story that alleged she had been paid by a Hindu nationalist politician to retract her statement against the accused. Instantly Zahira became an iconic figure of resistance and celebrated as a young Muslim woman willing to speak truth to power. Subsequently, the National Human Rights Commission successfully petitioned the Supreme Court of India to set aside the acquittal and secured a retrial of her case outside Gujarat. During the retrial in 2004, Zahira retracted her statement once again, saying that she had been forced by human rights activists to give false testimony, and reverted to her earlier version that she had seen nothing. As did other members of her family. The prosecution declared her a hostile witness. In 2005, the Supreme Court sentenced her to a year in prison for perjury.

The highest court of India sent a young Muslim woman who lost nine members of her family in a pogrom to jail. Given that survivors like Zahira Sheikh, supported by top human rights activists and with access to the highest court in India, could be manipulated by multiple actors, including Hindu nationalist politicians, in full view of the media and the court, one can imagine the vulnerability of poor Muslim witnesses who were brought to the courts by JF. Zahira's case should have been the canary in the mine. It should have given pause to activists who wanted to use the law against the state because it was a clear example that legal proceedings could itself be a form of minoritization. The witness could be transformed into a "self-condemned liar" in the courtroom. The different avatars of the Muslim witness—iconic victim, star witness, and finally a public liar—is also the trajectory of a survivor losing her voice as her legal case takes on a life of its own.

This media trial showed that the Hindu nationalist regime would not remain indifferent to activist efforts of using the law against it but would in fact mobilize its control over the legal infrastructure, including the courts, the police, and the prosecutors to teach Muslims *and* the activists helping them a lesson. In 2005, Zahira Sheikh was sentenced to jail for a year. In 2014, the Gujarat government filed a police complaint against the human rights activist and NGO that had helped Zahira and other Muslim witnesses. Efforts for justice in the aftermath of 2002 were polarized along the same lines that produced a one-sided attack against Muslims in the first place. This meant that for Muslim survivors living and working beside Hindus in the aftermath of violence would necessarily entail compromise, not ideological purity, as envisioned by activists. Muslims as a sizeable minority in Gujarat, like elsewhere in India, lived beside Hindu neighbors, customers, and businesses. And many Muslims, after an initial period of retreat and refuge in Muslim-majority neighborhoods, had no choice but to return to working and living beside the people who had harmed them.

Beyond Victims and Perpetrators

Going to the courts for Muslims often meant that they would have to identify their Hindu neighbors before a judge. This was dangerous because they could not rely on the police to protect them from reprisals. But it involved other kinds of risks as well. Risks that were embedded in the everyday social relationships that entangled Hindus and Muslims. Anti-impunity's focus on individual prosecution—and the language of victims versus perpetrators—meant that they worked with a snapshot of the Muslim as a victim. As the trials dragged on over several years, the survivors found themselves in new and unforeseen relationships vis-à-vis their neighbors, who had in the past looted their houses, broken their graveyard, or burned their shop.

Ziba Apa, a Muslim woman who was well respected in her neighborhood, recognized several Hindu neighbors in the mob that burned her tiny tin-roof shack. But she refused to testify against her neighbors. When I asked her about this decision, she told me that they—both Hindus and Muslims—were fighting the Ahmedabad Municipal Corporation to legalize electricity in their "illegal" squatter colony. Hindus approached her when they had "gutter problems" (related to sewage), and both neighborhoods suffered from the lack of basic amenities like water. A lot had changed since her neighbors had burned her shack. When I asked her if her neighbors felt remorse, she said "there was no way to see inside their heart." She had decided to work together with her Hindu neighbors on pressing issues that affected their common life. "To fight a case now, will be a betrayal," she said.

When Muslim survivors abandoned their legal cases, or retracted their statements in the courtroom, they became "hostile" witnesses, and it was construed as a major defeat for JF. "Compromise" was a fraught topic in legal review meetings. Lawyers would blame the paralegals for not keeping a tab on the survivor or blame the witness for not being strong enough to speak the truth or embellishing their statement with details and facts that did not corroborate with their "original" statements. The paralegals, who lacked a legal degree and could therefore always be dismissed as ignorant of the law, tried to explain the relationships that comprised the witness's life outside the courtroom. Muslims as not only victims of the pogrom but also suffering from issues like poverty, unemployment, and chronic illness did not fit the agenda of anti-impunity activism. For Muslims, the legal process did not address the fraught issue of living together beside the people who have harmed you. The idea of the victim was fixed, but the life of the survivor was fluid; the pogrom was state-sanctioned but also involved intimates who were known to each other.

Consider another example of the context under which Muslim witnesses were expected to fight for justice. In 2010, I met a witness, Abdul, along with a JF lawyer and paralegal. We parked our motorbike outside his shop, which was burned down in in 2002. Even though the lawyer and the paralegal were there to talk about his upcoming deposition, something else was on his mind. Newspapers were full of news about police and paramilitary forces roaming the city to brace for a legal decision on a controversial issue regarding Hindus and Muslims, a landmark legal case that could create widespread sectarian violence. It was around the demolition of a mosque by Hindu nationalists that they claimed was built on a temple. Now after countless adjournments, the courts were supposedly going to give a final decision. Regardless, the word on the street was clear—if the courts decided in favor of Hindus, peace would reign, but if they gave a decision in favor of Muslims, far-right Hindu groups would create "trouble," a codeword for attacks on Muslims.

ABDUL: What will happen tomorrow? I have rebuilt this shop out of nothing. With God's blessing, it is doing even better than what it used to in 2002. But this time we are taking no chances. I have not stocked any raw materials for two days. If something happens to my shop, I don't want to lose my stock along with everything else.

As I was leaving Abdul's shop, Bharatbhai pointed out some men sitting in a small room at the back. Did you see that man with henna-colored hair sitting at the back? I had noticed some men at the back of the shop but not paid attention. I found out that one of the men sitting behind the shop was an accused in a 2002-related case. Perhaps he was just a customer enjoying a cold drink. Perhaps, perhaps not. But what is key here is to know that the same witness who was expected to testify against his neighbors in the court-room was also running a business beside Hindus who may have participated in attacks on Muslims elsewhere. These men were well known and lived in the same neighborhood as the witnesses, and therefore Muslims were vul-nerable to repeated violence. Abdul's fears about his shop were well founded.

In 2011, a year after Abdul turned hostile in the courtroom, his grocery shop was attacked again, this time as part of what was called a "communal clash" in the mainstream newspapers but was a criminal attack on Muslim shops by a well-known Hindu bootlegger.[16] None of this vulnerability of being Muslim in Gujarat could be incorporated into anti-impunity's imagi-nation of the heroic individual victim. In conditions of violence between neighbors, where the violence is not simply an isolated event but linked inextricably to the process of becoming a minority, the binaries of silence versus forgetting and impunity versus justice do not account for collusion, even silence and forgetting, that may be necessary for survivors to live together with their neighbors.[17]

Conclusion

In the summer of 2013, I attended a meeting of activists on the lawns of the Gujarat *Vidyapeeth*, a large public university in Ahmedabad, where I saw many old and new faces, including those who had worked with Muslim sur-vivors. On that day they were planning an Ahmedabad version of the One Billion Rising women's march. It soon became clear to me that the funding and focus of their NGOs had moved away from the pogrom to new areas like children's education and domestic violence.

After the meeting ended, Niaza Apa, a middle-aged Muslim NGO worker, told the group that when she went to neighborhoods where many poor Hin-dus and Muslims had been recently relocated by the government to make the Sabarmati Riverfront, the auto drivers that ferried people around in shared taxis asked whether she "wanted to go to Hindustan [India] or Paki-stan." Like Juhapura, a massive Muslim ghetto called "Mini-Pakistan," the city was sprouting more ghettos, and the wall between Hindus and Muslims had only grown higher and stronger in the aftermath of the pogrom. She also mentioned other signs of Hindu becoming the norm in public spaces—Hindu temples inside police stations, the naming of government schemes after Hindu gods and goddesses, and the proliferation of Hindu symbols in public offices.

It was this process of the consolidation of Hindu supremacy in public culture and statecraft that was not addressed by procedural activism. The larger question of the minoritization of Muslims inside and outside the courtroom could not be asked from inside anti-impunity efforts to punish individual Hindus. The efforts of JF to use the law against the Gujarat government seem to reinforce the paradoxical status of the law, both as an instrument of the dominant and a resource for the marginalized to challenge that very dominance.[18] Indeed, one could make an argument that legal activism in landmark cases impeded the Hindu nationalist government's efforts to completely disregard the legal process. In some cases, legal trials did expose police bias and the government's efforts to subvert the legal process.

My point is that efforts to restore the rule of law in the aftermath of political violence are unable to account for the law itself as the terrain for the making of minorities. Justice First and its reliance on the courts show that in the very act of exposing illegality and impunity, human rights activists reinforced the powerlessness of Muslims in Gujarat. Muslim witnesses had survived a collective state-sanctioned attack but stood alone in the dock to prove that it had happened. Anti-impunity activism also failed to consider the violent intimacy of Muslims and Hindus living beside each other. The dichotomies that guided anti-impunity activism—resistance versus oppression, the rule of law versus violence, victim versus perpetrator, and impunity versus justice—combined with its faith in the rule of law as a neutral tool to empower the survivor failed to imagine a form of justice that would go beyond the law.

CHAPTER FOUR

Beyond the Unspeakable

IT IS COMMON TO ENCOUNTER TALK of "the invisible" and "the unspeakable" in the aftermath of sexual violence. For example, one of the first human rights reports that addressed sexual violence against Muslim women during the Gujarat pogrom opens by acknowledging the women-survivors "who had the will to live, and the courage to speak of the unspeakable." In turn, anthropologists, along with NGO workers and activists, take upon themselves the urgent task of "giving voice" to victims of sexual violence. But these notions raise important, if paradoxical, questions, like how to speak of the unspeakable. In Gujarat, there were several efforts by activists, students, NGOs, scholars, and journalists to unveil sexual violence.

In 2008, I was a part of such an effort when I accompanied a team of human rights activists to hear the testimony of a young Muslim woman, Shahana. We stood inside a small barber shop listening to her describe how her family was attacked by a Hindu mob. She was twenty-two years old when she saw her Hindu neighbors fill the street outside her house "like beads on a necklace, until not an inch of the road was visible." The activists were meeting Shahana because she was one of those "rare women" willing to talk about sexual violence. Over the course of an hour, she described a chilling account of how her family—the only Muslim family—in a predominantly Hindu neighborhood was nearly burned alive by their neighbors.

As Shahana and her mother tried to escape the mob, her mother stumbled while trying to scale the wall in their backyard through which her sisters and father had already left. The mob caught up with them. They knocked Shahana down, pulled her *dupatta* (scarf worn around the shoulders that also covers the upper body), and tried to tear her clothes off. At this point, Shahana paused, abused the mob, and challenged them to confront her *now*. "What would have happened that day if I hadn't escaped?"

Even as I felt the force of her question, I noticed that she did not expect an answer and neither did any of the activists press her on the point. As we were leaving the barbershop, the JF lawyer and paralegal in charge of her case told the human rights team that the accused in her case were acquitted of all charges. During the trial, Shahana's mother had told the judge that the accused tried to rape her daughter, but there was no mention of rape in the case and neither did Shahana use the word in the courtroom. In the end, the judge found Shahana and her mother's testimony "inconsistent and contradictory" and dismissed the charges. Nothing new in this. A vast body of feminist literature on rape and rape trials show that such trials most often end in acquittals.

In fact, the paralegals and lawyers were not surprised by the acquittal. They pointed out that there were multiple contradictions in what Shahana had said at different points of time to different audiences: before activists in public hearings, before the police when they had taken her statement, and then before the judge in the courtroom. The underlying premise of their argument was clear even if they did not say it in as many words: there was no sexual violence to expose. They told me that this was not a good case of sexual violence at all. Put differently, there was something about Shahana's case that did not fit the genre of sexual violence testimony, something about her tone of telling and mode of showing that did not fit with the image of the victim. For me this pointed to something inadequate about the model of exposure that we—activist, lawyer, and anthropologist—were using to hear her. What did we want to hear? How could we recognize sexual violence when we saw it?

After Shahana finished telling her story, the head of the human rights team asked her pointed questions to corroborate the details of her testimony: What time did she see the men? What were the men carrying? Does she know the names of the accused? When did she report the case to the police? Unsurprisingly, her answers confirmed a familiar pattern in most 2002-related cases. The police refused to file a complaint. They incited the Hindu mob to burn her house. In addition, her Hindu neighbors who attacked her family live only a few houses away from her.

One could analyze this case as one more example of the legal erasure of sexual violence. But this assumes that sexual violence is a stable object and that the task of the anthropologist is to make it visible and then counter its erasure by the state and the patriarchal logics that flow through the courts, community, and society. This erasure theory of sexual violence also places the listener and speaker (and the anthropologist) in a familiar triangle: the female victim (speaker), the all-powerful patriarchal State (actor), and the analyst (listener) who recovers the unspeakable from testimony. But something in Shahana's narrative frustrated this mode of exposure—and the attempts by human rights activists and lawyers to uncover hidden sexual violence and disclose it before the law. "It was not a good case." My point is that Shahana's case is a good case to understand sexual violence precisely because it is also a tale of a survivor resisting the exposure of sexual violence in terms that insert them into familiar subject positions like "the rape victim" that further harm them. Precisely because it was not a good case of sexual violence for the activist and the lawyer that it makes it a good case for me to illustrate both the limits of exposure and the need to compose sexual violence not as some unique, unspeakable act that is too terrible to be represented but as part of a wider practice of overlapping words and actions that mark the scene of minoritization itself.

What I present here is not another story of how patriarchal courts, families, and communities erase sexual violence, but a mode of composing sexual violence that can give an account of its persistence, dispersal, and proliferation inside and outside the courtroom as a constitutive aspect of the minoritization of Muslims. In other words, in contexts of mass violence, like Gujarat 2002, there is a tension between our familiar language of erasure to analyze sexual violence and its widespread circulation in media and public culture. This paradox became clear to me when the head of the human rights team remarked in a meeting that sexual violence in Gujarat was both the most talked about and least analyzed aspect of the pogrom. I use this paradox to show the limits of using the law to expose sexual violence as well as the possibility of composing sexual violence as constitutive of the experience of being a minority.

In other words, what do we do with sexual violence in conditions of visibility? In such a context, the challenge is no longer to make the invisible visible but to ask why terms like erasure and invisibility attach themselves to sexual violence *despite* it being so widespread. Why does sexual violence persist in testimony, human rights reports, scholarly accounts, rumors, and the courtroom and yet remain chiefly understood as unspeakable? And then, how do we compose accounts of sexual violence that place it within a longer arc of what it means to be a Muslim and stand before police, the judge, and even your neighbors? To answer these questions, I suggest we take a break from breaking silences, uncovering the erased, and speaking the unspeakable. No doubt it is important to find forms that make the unspeakable knowable and shareable.[1] But that is a not the path I took because I wanted to respect the silence of the people and communities I met in Gujarat. So I focus on what is said, what surrounds all that is said, and the effects of what is said. By doing so, I find terms like exaggeration that can help us understand how sexual violence persists under conditions of simultaneous erasure and visibility. For example, in Shahana's testimony, which I analyze in more detail later, the physical attack on Shahana is not the beginning or end of sexual violence, and neither is she the only target, even though activists and the law would like to narrate sexual violence as an unspeakable event. Rather, one finds that Muslim women are targeted by the police, a rioting mob, and later neighbors in ways that show that the sexual violence is part of a wider process of constituting them as minority subjects.

Feminist work argues that representations of sexual violence run the risk of deepening tropes of victimhood and may require a break from feminist positions. As Janet Halley writes, "while feminism is committed to affirming and identifying itself with female injury, it may thereby, unintentionally, intensify it."[2] One way to take such a break would be a move away from the obsession with a traumatic event and pay more attention to the everyday life of the survivor.[3] Nayanika Mookherjee critiques "hegemonic aesthetic narratives" like the horrific sublime that are deployed by feminists and activists to understand rape victims. She goes on to say that the "idea of trauma [i.e., not trauma itself] in fact freezes time; it arrests the dynamics and contradictions of experience, subject formation and agency, and becomes a rigid mode condemned to repetition."[4] Crucially, then, a too strong focus on the traumatic event may flatten the survivor's experience of sexual violence and the way it is folded into the everyday.[5] In discussing the fraught relationship between the law and feminist responses to sexual violence, Nivedita Menon argues that the apparent universality of sexual violence actually rests on assumptions about sex and the body, for instance the assumption that sexuality is the "truest, deepest expression of selfhood" and that these assumptions can often support the patriarchal values that feminists attack elsewhere in their work.[6] Like the idea that sexual violence is a unique form of violence that violates women in some fundamental way. These assumptions are also the basis for constituting sexual violence as something fundamentally unspeakable.

I suggest that we compose accounts of sexual violence that do not seek to unveil something unspeakable by means of a renewed engagement with forms of visibility. Like making a map of sexual violence that is not oriented toward a spot marked by X, most often rape, but a story of how sexual violence is discussed, represented, circulated, but dismissed in the aftermath; a story in which the survivor is neither a victim nor heroic but part of a wider attack on Muslim men, women, and children.

In her study of public violence in Argentina, Diana Taylor writes, "my goal is to make visible again, not the invisible or imagined, but that which is clearly there but not allowed to be seen."[7] Elizabeth Drexler while analyzing official documents of state violence in Aceh writes that "in contrast to filling in silences, exploration of logics and form reveal both the conditions in which silencing and violence become possible and how certain disclosures fail to produce accountability."[8] I build on these approaches that seek to work with what is clearly there but not allowed to be seen to outline the effects of what happens when Muslim women *do* speak before the police, the judge, and the activist. Such a map outlines the contours of sexual violence not as a stable object within testimony (was the survivor raped or not?) but as a form of language that persists across institutions and archives far beyond the Event. I offer the term exaggeration to track the persistence of sexual violence across a range of sites of violence and its redress by activists, courts, and the state. By tracking the transformation of sexual violence into exaggeration, sexual violence is more than a story of visibility and invisibility. Instead, I suggest that sexual violence proliferates as rumor and verbal or physical abuse, is inscribed on the walls of Muslim houses, is a threat used by the police to prevent Muslims from registering complaints, and is woven into the everyday life of Muslim women. In other words, far from being a dark and invisible force, sexual violence follows the survivor into new spaces and situations beyond the pogrom. The question, then, is no longer why sexual violence is erased, but what are the forms in which it persists across sites as disparate as the Indian parliament, the courtroom, human rights activism and reports, and mainstream media. To do so, I pay attention to the police report, the proximity of the police station to the scene of violence, the intimacy of the Hindu neighbors to the Muslim women they attacked, the words they used to sexualize them, and how this persistence marks the category of the minority.

"The Courage to Speak the Unspeakable"

Why do notions of silence, invisibility, and the unsayable come to define discussions of sexual violence? The feminist and activist reports I analyze in this section symbolize a tension between the visibility and invisibility of sexual violence. Even as activists set out to record victims' testimony of sexual violence in Gujarat, they ended up tracking its erasure at multiple sites and by multiple actors. This entanglement of erasure and expression, the pain of the victim and the pleasures of the perpetrator run parallel to the problem I encountered and described while reading the police archive.[9] How does one read the archive of sexual violence if it is also simultaneously the archive of its erasure? One way around this problem is to look beyond the official archive. If we consider multiple sources of information about sexual violence: mainstream media, legal records, popular accounts including rumors, perpetrators bragging about torture, and eyewitness and witness testimony, then we face the challenge of having to arrange very different kinds of affects, practices, and sites into a coherent object called sexual violence that is at the same time absent and present.

Activist reports argue that sexual violence during the pogrom becomes invisible and unspeakable in large part due to patriarchal logics of shame and honor that prevent women from speaking about it and the state's refusal to acknowledge the widespread targeting of Muslim women and children. Therefore, anyone who speaks about sexual violence becomes a person who has the "courage to speak the unspeakable."[10] Such efforts to recover the unspeakable are a widespread response in the aftermath of mass violence and align with what may be called the recovery project of Subaltern studies—which tried to recover the voice and subjectivity of the subaltern. And yet recovery is not straightforward because what is sought to be recovered is unstable. One report writes that "women have suffered the most bestial forms of sexual violence—including rape, gang rape, mass rape, stripping, insertion of objects into their body, stripping, and molestations. A majority of the women who suffered this violence were then burnt alive."[11] Even though this description mentions rape, it acknowledges the wide range of actions that are part of "sexual violence."

The report opens by acknowledging the women "who had the will to live, and the courage *to speak the unspeakable*" (emphasis mine). It goes on to find "there is compelling evidence of sexual violence against women. These crimes against women have been grossly underreported and the exact extent of these crimes—in rural and urban areas—demands further investigation." Despite meeting and interviewing numerous survivors and human rights workers, the authors find only five detailed testimonies, but many more statements by witnesses. Put differently, while the activists "hear" of numerous rapes, there is "official evidence" for only one such incident in the entire district.

Here, what is important to note is that sexual violence takes forms that can be heard but are not legible to the law. So, the unspeakable is not always what is not spoken but what is not supported by evidence as defined by the law. For instance, sexual violence circulates widely as rumor. When accounts of sexual violence circulate unaccompanied by official evidence, then they are dismissed by state officials, politicians, and even mainstream media. The law minister and the prime minister of India argued that reports of sexual violence were exaggerated because, as the law minister told the Parliament, "only two FIRs [First Information Reports] have filed for rape in Gujarat so far." The search for sexual violence as a stable object supported by clear evidence is therefore a part of the problem of analyzing its prevalence, extent, and effects on survivors.

The activists reconcile this disjuncture between what they hear (the prevalence of sexual violence in various guises) with the absence of first-person testimony through the concept of invisibility. "In Panchmahals district only one rape FIR has been filed, though we heard of many other cases. There has been a complete invisibilisation of the issue of sexual violence in the media."[12] This means, however, that the invisibility of sexual violence is *not* uniform. In fact, there was a kind of sexual violence that was hypervisible. For instance, fictitious acts of rape of Hindu women by Muslims circulated in mainstream media and were printed on the front page of Gujarati newspapers. On February 28, the front page of the Gujarati newspaper *Sandesh* carried a fictitious report on the abduction and rape of Hindu women by Muslims in Godhra titled "Religious mob abducts 10–15 Hindu girls out of train bogies."[13] This report mentions that "In an act of inhumanity that would make even a devil weep, both girls had their breasts cut off. It is evident from the dead bodies that the victims had been repeatedly raped. There is speculation that the girls might have died because of gross sexual abuse."[14]

In response to such reports of fictitious attacks on Hindu women, activists write that "ironically, while false stories about the rape of Hindu women have done the rounds, there has been virtual silence in the media, including the English language papers, about the real stories of sexual violence against

Muslim women."[15] This is more than simply bad journalism. It helps us to understand that invisibility is not linked inextricably to sexual violence. And that the visibility of sexual violence is ethnicized in Gujarat; it becomes a mode of establishing the difference between Hindus and Muslims. The perpetrators of violence against Muslim women were only too happy to describe acts of torture, and in their accounts the violation of Muslim women is *not* unspeakable but shot through with pleasure and fantasy. As Tanika Sarkar noted, "the woman's body was a site of almost inexhaustible violence, with infinitely plural and creative forms of torture."[16] The widespread circulation of rumors and fantasies of sexual violence against Hindu women also acted as the template for attacks on Muslim women.[17]

The different ways in which violence against Hindu and Muslim women circulated during the pogrom shows that it is impossible to tackle the visibility/invisibility of sexual violence outside its place within a larger process of minoritization. And first-person testimony of rape is only one among many forms in which sexual violence becomes visible. For instance, the report mentions the media's "self-censorship about rape stories." It finds "senior journalists in Ahmedabad say that they can be accused of rumor mongering if they carry stories about rape, given that a bulk of the victims are either dead, or if alive have neither had medical examinations nor lodged FIRs." Again, the absence of sexual violence here is not a matter of the unspeakable. It is about the limited but dominant understanding of sexual violence as rape. And even when "rape stories" are in circulation, if they are not supported by a violated body, an official document, or a medical report, then they are transformed into rumors. Here medico-legal procedures used to establish rape, the paper trail of police documentation, and everyday legality structure who can speak and what can they speak about.

A second report on sexual violence in Gujarat prepared by an international committee of feminists tried to understand "sexual violence against women and how this can be effectively addressed by a legal system not equipped to deal with crimes of this nature and scale."[18] It emphasized, "Rapes were not the only form of sexual assault. There were many others like verbal abuses, molestation and taunts that continue till today and a humiliation that knows no bound."[19] This notion of violence beyond rape signals a temporality different from a singular, unspeakable event. In other words, as soon as we approach sexual violence beyond the unspeakable, a broader map of words and actions emerge; and the target of sexual violence is not the individual but the community. For instance, the report describes how the police would strip themselves before Muslim women to prevent them from defending their houses and their families. If we categorize these acts as sexual violence, their target is not only women and their bodies, but their ability to resist the attack on Muslim property.

The report further breaks down the silence surrounding sexual violence into different parts. Some women choose to keep silent "because it is shameful to proclaim sexual violence against one's own body in traditional ethos. In the patriarchal family structure and system of values, the violation of women's bodily integrity becomes a source of shame not only for the women as individuals but for them as members/symbols of family and community."[20]

The Paroli case is a good example to understand how efforts to make sexual violence visible can get entangled with patriarchal dynamics of shame and honor. A decade after a Hindu mob attacked Miyanbhai as well as his son and two daughters, Justice First got a sense that he was no longer interested in going to court. The summary of his case was as follows. A large Hindu mob had gathered, but only a few of them physically attacked them. The mob attacked the whole family with wooden sticks and metal pipes, broke the hand of his wife, knifed his son, and hit one of his daughters with a pipe and broke her hand. In an interview Miyanbhai had said, almost in passing, that the mob molested (*ched chad kiya*) his second daughter. When some of the men started pursuing his girls, someone in the mob said, "leave the girls alone, don't harass them." Sometime during the attack, the two girls tried to escape into the fields. At some point, the parents lost track of their daughters and fell unconscious. And when they regained consciousness in the evening they were on the road. They spent the day in the fields. Some unknown person told the police about them and they were picked up the next day. After the attack, one of the girls had become silent and numb. Initially, when the paralegal had asked Miyanbhai what happened, he had said that nothing happened. Later he added, "They disrobed her but someone, we don't know who, shouted loudly and scattered the mob."

This refusal of Miyanbhai and his family to fight their legal case was construed by Justice First as a major failure. To understand Miyanbhai's refusal to pursue his case, I accompanied Ustadbhai, a JF paralegal assigned with the task of persuading the witness not to compromise with the accused. Compromise, whether mentioned or not by the witness, was always the chief cause for a witness to withdraw their case.

In the Paroli case, like Shahana's case, there was no sexual violence "on record" since the family had refused to disclose the molestation of their daughter to the police. Miyanbhai and his wife had made it clear to Justice First that they did *not* want the names of the daughters to appear anywhere in the courtroom. Off the record, they had acknowledged that during the attack they were separated from their daughters and one daughter was molested.

When we met Miyanbhai, the father of the daughters, in his house, his wife made her displeasure explicit by meeting us without exchanging greetings. The daughters, who were also there, maintained their distance from us. It was striking that we never exchanged a word with the women. Ustadbhai tried his best over a couple of hours to persuade Miyanbhai to keep fighting for his rights in the court. It slowly emerged that his resolve to fight the case had been weakened by the fear of his daughter's name coming up during the trial. Even though the JF lawyer had promised that *he* would not bring it up during the trial, he had also said that since the "incident" was known in the village, and the injury certificate of the women was on the record, the defense lawyers could always ask questions about his daughters. The trial could turn into public humiliation.[21] In the legal review meeting, senior lawyers in Ahmedabad had disagreed with the local lawyer and said that the defense would not want to bring it up for fear of raising questions about police complicity. Miyanbhai was wary of a trial where the defense lawyers could potentially drag his daughters to the courtroom to cross-examine them about the details of the molestation. The JF lawyer had warned him that all kind of questions could be asked in the court, like "where was his hand?" "Where did he place his leg?"

The object sexual violence is under erasure here not only from state institutions but from within the family and community of the survivor. And the politics of exposure cannot avoid the possibility that exposure may invite further violence. Initially, there could be no mention of the molestation because the girls were young. Now, a decade later, there could still be no mention of the molestation because the survivor had been married off and the in-laws could send her back if they heard about the attack. Miyanbhai was worried that the in-laws had heard rumors about additional compensation money for riot victims and were demanding the share due to the daughters-in-law. During the three-hour-long conversation between Ustadbhai and Miyanbhai, I witnessed a struggle to find a way to expose violence but keep sexual violence hidden. It was clear that simply speaking about sexual violence, making it visible, would not undo the structures of power and domination that would frame the survivor as soon as she entered the dock.

Targeting the Body

On March 1 at 12 a.m., a police inspector wrote an "omnibus" FIR describing the violence in the neighborhood where Shahana and her family live: "After post Godhra Episode, VHP had called Gujarat *Bandh* and accordingly the city was under tense [*sic*] and the complainant himself was patrolling. Since the situation was not within control and *mobs of both the castes* were causing physical atrocities to each other the curfew was imposed . . . it was reported that there was heavy stone pelting *from both sides*" (emphasis mine).

Thereafter the report describes the police *moving* through the neighborhood quelling "mob violence," responding to wireless messages, and using tear gas and batons to disburse riotous crowds. Unsurprisingly, it does not describe any specific event of murder, looting, and arson against Muslims. Instead, it mentions the names of forty persons, both Hindus and Muslims, and two witnesses, Shahana and her mother. Compare, now, the actions of the police in Shahana's testimony. In Shahana's narrative to the human rights team, the police are key instigators of the attacks.

The local police inspector (PI) Joshi was "patrolling the area" and passed Shahana's house, as the mob outside her house got ready to burn it down. Shahana jumped in front of his jeep and urged him to come out and stop the mob. He stopped and stepped out of the jeep, turned to the mob, and said, "what are you waiting for, burn these f*****s!" During the attacks the family was separated for six days and reunited only at the relief camp. When they returned, a temple with idols of Hindu gods (*Jognimata* and *Hanuman*) was installed at the spot where their house used to be. Shahana and her father made many trips to the police station, which is opposite their house, to file a complaint. The police abused them and refused to file a complaint for ten days. "You are still alive? How did you manage that?" asked Amaliar, the police officer in charge of the Gomalipur police station. When her father replied, "it's all in *His* hands," the police hit him with a baton. "Give us proof that you lived there," the police told them when they tried to report the destruction of their house and the construction of a makeshift "temple" on it. On the tenth day, a tall and light-eyed police officer told the others, "This girl has been coming here for ten days, whether you want to do something or not, at least take her complaint?" They finally took her "handwritten" complaint on April 5. There is no trace of this complaint in the police record. When Shahana shouted at the police officers for hitting them, they told her father, "Your daughter talks too much, tell her to shut up, or I'll shove my stick in her mouth."

As we heard Shahana tell this story, she paused before she recalled the abuses used by the police. They dislodged her from the flow of her story. "The police here have openly abused Muslim women; they have used every abuse they know for Muslims on us. This is the state of the police here," she said. When Shahana's family returned home from the relief camp, they saw "unmentionable abuses" written on the walls of their house. Even though Shahana chose not to describe the abuses in front of the human rights team, we can get a sense of what she saw scribbled on the walls from fact-finding committees that visited Gujarat in the aftermath. An all-women fact-finding committee was shown video footage where "they saw slogans like—Muslims Quit India—or we will f*** your mothers—written on the walls of charred houses."[22]

I want to draw attention here to the range of words and actions that target Shahana's body—the police beat her when she tries to lodge a complaint, a Hindu mob disrobes her, the police use sexual abuse to intimidate her, a policeman threatens "to shove his stick" in her mouth, and finally sexual abuses are inscribed on the walls of their house. The mob's attempt to disrobe Shahana was not the end of sexual violence, but rather it began a series of attacks on her body and her family. While Shahana and her mother were waiting for the trial, one of the accused stabbed her mother. And long after the pogrom has ended, when Shahana still lived in the same neighborhood as the accused, Hindu men exposed themselves before her and her sister when they used the nearby public toilets.

The Appearance of Rape

On September 12, 2008, Shahana's mother deposed before a judge. She described the scene outside her verandah after she finished her prayers that day. She named six accused (one had a can of kerosene in his hand) as part of a mob of twenty-five men. One of them poured fuel on the shop, and the others torched it with burning sticks. They proceeded to loot the barber shop next to the house, where the dowry of her three daughters was stored, and finally burned down the shop and the house before her eyes. Later when she fled her house, one of the accused stabbed her, and she turned around to see that "the mob had knocked her daughter Shahana down, was abusing her badly, and tried to rape her."

This is the *first* appearance of rape in this case.

Despite all attempts by the police, prosecution, and even JF lawyers to sidestep the mob's assault on Shahana, her mother's testimony forces it out in the open and leaves an indelible mark on the trial. The effects of uttering rape, however, are paradoxical. Rape dissolves the trial, which, until Shahana's mother's testimony, had officially—on record—nothing to do with sexual violence. When I asked JF paralegals and lawyers about her mother's testimony, they said, "She [Shahana's mother] got emotional, and spoke more than necessary."

What did prosecution lawyers and the judge do with the utterance of rape? In other words, this is not a question about the invisibility of rape but its weaponization by the law against Muslims.

Since rape is nowhere in her previous statements to the police, the defense lawyers during the cross-examination asked Shahana's mother why she did not report this to the police. She answered, "In my complaint, the police wrote down what I said except certain statements. The police did not record the attempt to rape my daughter and the can of kerosene carried by the accused." Like other cases, allegations by witnesses that the police did not accurately record their statement produced a standard response from defense lawyers. Did the witness then make any "written applications" to any official agency—magistrate or police commissioner are the two recognized authorities—to place on record their correct statement? In other words, did the witness have any documents to prove why they didn't have documents?

In response, Shahana's mother said, "I did not file any application that the police did not write my complaint according to my wishes. . . . It is true that the rape attempt on my daughter is not mentioned in my police complaint. It is true that the police station is right opposite my house." With these words her cross-examination ended.

Shahana deposed three days after her mother but she did not utter the word rape. A schoolgirl at the time of the assault, she was now married and a mother of a young girl. Like her mother, she described how she watched the accused burn her house and shop. And then she told the judge, "The men [in the courtroom today] sitting here knocked me on the ground" (*mane dhakka marinay neeche pade dhigale*). Somehow my mother and I escaped them and fled."

Her cross-examination followed a familiar arc: the defense noted that her deposition was different from the police statement. Like her mother, she said, "It is true that my police statement does not mention that the accused knocked me on the ground or that he was leading the mob." Shahana's cross-questioning ended with the telling statement that "it is true that the police station is 25–30 steps away from my house."

In both cross-examinations, the proximity of the scene of violence to the police station is a key point emphasized by the defense. This emphasis on the distance between the scene of violence and the scene of the law is the first turn in the key that will turn the witness's testimony against the witness. In her analysis of the limits of representing rape, Ananya Jahanara Kabir points out that "if keeping silent about rape constitute one set of problems, I want to suggest that speaking about rape sets into motion a different problematic by upsetting the delicately poised nature of the subject as a 'public secret.'"[23] I want to suggest that the utterance of the "unspeakable" is given the same treatment as other testimony by Muslims, and the legal trial turns testimony against the Muslim witness. Defense lawyers and then the judge frame the targeting of Muslim women as a question of timing and documentation. Rape becomes a weapon for the judge and the defense to cast a doubt on the entire case and the credibility of the witnesses.

"The Dust of Doubt"

On September 17, 2008, six years after Shahana and her family were attacked and their house burned down before their eyes, the accused in her case were acquitted. "The evidence which is tendered by the prosecution is suffering from the [*sic*] basic infirmities and improvement which is not found to be free from the dust of doubt and therefore, this Court hesitates in holding the accused persons guilty to the charge," concluded the judge in his twelve-page judgment.

What "basic infirmities and improvement" were found by the defense and the judge in this case? The judge found Shahana and her mother "exaggerated their deposition and their evidence recorded on oath is not found to be consistent with the case of the prosecution." The exaggeration is that they have "*given two inconsistent statement* [sic] *about one fact* for which reasonable doubt arises in the mind of the court" (emphasis mine). This one fact is of course the attack on Shahana. In other words, sexual violence does cross the threshold of the law. The law is not blind to it, but spots it as a weakness, transforms it into an exaggeration, a hammer to smash the entire case with. In response to Shahana's mother's testimony in court that the police did not accurately record her statement, the judge describes their encounter with the police:

These two witnesses have been tested by searching cross-examination. These witnesses have admitted that fact that the attempt to commit the rape has not been disclosed by them before the police. The facts stated by them in examination-in-chief have not stated [*sic*] before the police.

Note here that disclosure and not erasure is the key issue. And this is not only the lack of disclosure before the police but the lack of disclosure at the right time and the right place. The judgment draws attention to the belatedness of the accusation:

> It is worth to mention that the incident has taken place in the month of February 2002 and the statement of these witnesses came to be reported by the Investigating Agency in the month of April 2002 with inordinate delay. When their statement came to be recorded by the police they were lodged with the relief camp. No immediate F.I.R. has been lodged by P.W.9 and P.W.10 for the alleged loss caused to them by the accused persons.

It is not only *what* was said, but *before* whom it was said, and *when* was it said that is at stake here. To be credible, the witnesses can only repeat the police version of what happened. If, however, they say what is outside the paper trail, then it is false because it is inconsistent with the record. This bind, as I have shown elsewhere, is not limited to sexual violence but affects all Muslim witnesses. Let me ask here the question that the judge did not: What did it mean to be a Muslim and stand before the police during the pogrom? What happened to Muslim women on the street, in the relief camp, and inside the police station?

From the entire evidence of testimonial literature, including human rights reports and official inquiry commissions, being *before the police* is in fact part of the fear, abuse, and humiliation experienced by Muslims in Gujarat. From Shahana's narrative, we know that the police were not merely passive bystanders who failed to provide protection to the only Muslim house and shop in the entire neighborhood, but instigated and supervised the attack on her house. "Delay" in reporting becomes "material improvement." In the chapter on the police archive, I have discussed the temporality of police documentation during the pogrom and why so few survivors could register complaints with the police. Refusal by the police, curfew, and the continuing attacks on Muslims over several months are a few of the many reasons why such a delay may be justifiable.

What happens during the trial is that the judge and the defense lawyers seize the utterance of rape to cast a shadow on the witness. The defense and the judge cannot dismiss the burned house and shop, nor can they ignore the names of the people mentioned by the witness. Instead, they compose a new scene of violence. The judge utilizes the category of the "mob" to justify the presence of the accused at the crime scene. This is noteworthy because the original police statement does mention the presence of the accused (only the names, not their actions) and the judge cannot disregard this vital piece of "documentary" evidence. Therefore, the judge argues, "The mob may be gathered [*sic*] to see as to what is happening. Simply because the accused persons were present in the mob, it cannot be said that they were members of unlawful assembly." Such Kafkaesque reversals are key achievements of the trial: the survivor becomes the accused, and the accused becomes the witness. Not to belabor the point, but this is a dynamic that cannot be explained through categories of erasure and invisibility. The judge does not stop at questioning the credibility of the witnesses; he attributes specific motivations to them: "Perhaps some ill feeling or because of *communal feeling* the witnesses have preferred to exaggerate the prosecution version." Shahana and her mother's testimony, according to the judge, are motivated by ulterior—communal—motives. At one level, the judgment is a tried and tested template for dismissing the testimony of Muslim witnesses, repeated across courts in Ahmedabad, replete with terms like contradiction, improvement, and inconsistency. But the court's use of exaggeration to describe the utterance of rape has a robust life outside the courtroom.

The Logic of Exaggeration

Rape, torture, and bodily forms of cruelty against women are much discussed features of political violence in South Asia. Disbelief and accusations of exaggeration typically follow such accounts. While describing the experience of women during the Partition of India in 1947, feminist scholars felt that context and commentary needed to be added to women's narratives because without it their testimonies would be exposed to "charges of exaggeration."[24] Like the Partition of India and subsequent communal riots, Muslim women's bodies in Gujarat were a site for men to violate and protect community honor. Soon after the news of the massacre spread across India, stories of Hindu mobs raping, stripping, burning, and maiming Muslim women became one of the most striking aspects of the pogrom.

Responding to these narratives of violence against Muslim women in the Indian Parliament, George Fernandes, the then defense minister of India said, "There is nothing new in the mayhem let loose in Gujarat. . . .

A pregnant woman's stomach being slit, a daughter being raped in front of a mother isn't a new thing. . . . Such things have been happening for 54 years in India and happened even on the streets of New Delhi in 1984."[25] Notice that the minister recognizes sexual violence but normalizes it as *mere* repetition, as a routine aspect of politics, whereby any attention to it for its own sake becomes unnecessary, even an exaggeration.[26]

One incident in Gujarat became a symbol of the brutality of the pogrom. A local leader of the *Bajrang Dal*, a militant Hindu nationalist organization, bragged on camera about how he attacked and ripped open the stomach of a pregnant woman,[27] paraded the fetus on the tip of a sword, and later "called up the home minister and went to sleep."[28] Supporters of the Hindu nationalist government claimed that this woman was a creation of the media. For human rights reports, like *The Survivor's Speak*, Kausar Bano became a "meta narrative of bestiality" and "helpless victimhood." Due to the efforts of the national English media, feminist human rights teams, and the activists supporting, the case led to a landmark judgment that recognized sexual violence. But the question of exaggeration never disappeared.[29] In a section titled, "Exaggerations," the judge regards aspects of the survivor's testimony as exaggeration and "embroidery" that may be there but cannot be used to dismiss the entirety of the testimony.

Sexual violence is an integral part of the violence that founded India. In the context of the Partition of India, feminist scholars have analyzed the abduction of women and their subsequent forcible "return" to India and Pakistan as important in the construction of the nation. Partition survivors have described the systematic targeting of women to "injure" and "humiliate" the community. Because communities view women as symbols of honor, mobs often use sexual violence as a tool to attack nation-states. These studies have also showed how the bodies of women became the space on which male rioters inscribed political slogans. Scholars and activists described similar patterns of violence against Muslim women during Gujarat 2002. During normal periods, the state separates normal from pathological women in rape trials to normalize sexual violence and to use the woman's body to read her "sexual past," rather than focusing on the protection of the bodily integrity of women.[30] The logic of exaggeration allows the law to both recognize and dismiss sexual violence in the same gesture.

Constructing a New Scene

I opened this chapter with a paradox: activists and anthropologists attempt to interrogate institutional modes of representing sexual violence while being attentive to the limits and effects of their own modes of enclosure.[31] This is the problem of how to write and read sexual violence as not the unspeakable, unthinkable, the exceptional, but as constitutive of the scene of political violence against minorities. In terms of fieldwork, it demands a mode of approaching the survivor beyond victimhood. I suggest that such an approach requires an attention to form, to the ways in which not only judges and the police but also activists and feminists create forms to make sexual violence intelligible. By paying attention to the different ways in which sexual violence appears, disappears, circulates, and persists inside and outside the courtroom, it is no longer an isolated, unspeakable act, something that begins and ends with rape. Instead, it opens the question of the centrality of sexual violence within the scene of political violence—as a weapon in the hands of the police, judge, and defense lawyers, as a mode of silencing the survivor, and as a technique to create the difference between majorities and minorities.

One way of paying attention to form is of course by experimenting with it. Consider the example of *The Lightning Testimonies* (2007), an eight-channel video installation on sexual violence in South Asia by the Indian filmmaker Amar Kanwar. The installation used eight projectors to concurrently display still and moving images on all walls of a darkened room in the Art Institute in Chicago. The effect was simultaneously alienating and immersive. Crackling campfire, thunder and rain, and close-ups of bright orange flowers mixed with testimonies of women affected by mass violence in South Asia, ranging from the Partition of India in 1947 to the anti-Muslim pogrom in 2002. As I struggled to make sense of Kanwar's provocative and disorienting composition of sexual violence, I became aware that rather than resolving the question of sexual violence into a single image, metaphor, event, or act, the installation was challenging the politics of visibility itself.

Watching Kanwar's installation, I found myself surrounded by luminous rectangles displaying scenes from everyday life in South Asia: a bonfire in Manipur, two men on a motorbike in Gujarat, sepia photographs, and newspaper articles in Bengali. Unlike conventional representations of sexual violence in academic and activist accounts, there was no introduction, no argument, and certainly no place from where I could see all eight channels at the same time. This fractured the power of the official archive to render sexual violence as mere "embroidery."

Other visitors seemed to be in a similar position: some, like me, sat on small white cubes in the center of the room. Others stood in corners, trying to watch more than one film. It was difficult to focus on any single projection or sound or to connect an image with its appropriate soundtrack because all eight video channels played simultaneously. This was similar to my feeling of listening to Shahana speak. I realized that *The Lightning Testimonies* was disorienting because it never gave the viewer a victim or an event. Instead, it kept interrupting the viewer's search for a body by incorporating memory and landscape and mood as part of the narrative of sexual violence itself. I recalled my experience of listening to Shahana; at one point she challenged the men who attacked her to appear before her to settle scores, and at another time she shuddered when she recalled in her mind the words the police hurled at her.

In fact, narrative may not be a good description of what happens in the installation. Ananya Jahanara Kabir argues that it is precisely the non-narrative and nonlinguistic perspective offered by *The Lightning Testimonies* that "enable[s] the most ethical form of representation possible."[32] The installation presented the testimony of survivors but reframed their stories outside of individual experience. Instead, the experience was embedded in images of trees, clouds, rain, and weaving—a shift from the forensic to the poetic. The eight videos moved from the register of the real (newspaper articles) to the performative (scenes from a play) and back again. Instead of uncovering a stable narrative of violation and victimhood, or even an object called sexual violence, the images slowed down, froze, and refused to focus on their object, thereby interrupting the audience's desire to see "the horror" and then move on.

My point here is not to present Kanwar's work as the solution to the question of what is sexual violence or to suggest that it is the true form to make the invisible visible, but to emphasize that *The Lightning Testimonies* asks a different question: What forms should activists and scholars use to compose sexual violence such that it is not a single, exceptional Event? Kanwar's film made me rethink the building blocks of the stories we tell about sexual violence. By focusing on the forests and birds that live around a scene of violence and the provisional and oblique strategies by which communities and witnesses respond to sexual violence, Kanwar's film presents the multiple temporalities of sexual violence as it enters the courtroom, is staged as part of a play, and woven into fabric of the communities that live to tell the tale. The images loop in and out, you see a shawl, a rock, a scene from a play, a barren landscape of mountains and stones, all of this together baffles the viewer and forces them to see sexual violence anew.

For example, one of the eight screens of Kanwar's film described the story of Bilkis Bano, a Muslim woman whose family was killed and who was gang-raped during the pogrom in Gujarat. The camera lingered on the dry and stony landscape, pausing with a wide shot of mountains in the distance. But soon the outline of those mountains, the dips, ridges, and peaks, began to plot the timeline of the legal case. Helped by activists, Bilkis pursued her case for five years: initially dismissed in the lower court, the case was transferred and then adjudicated outside Gujarat, ending with a conviction.[33] What would it mean to plot such a timeline for Shahana? Would it be a simple reversal of the Bilkis case because there was no conviction? Perhaps it would be composed of the words of the policeman who threatened to shove his baton down her mouth if she did not stop speaking, the gaze of the men who attempted to disrobe her but cannot look her in the eye, the abuses inscribed on the walls of her house that are now inscribed in her mind, her neighbors exposing themselves while they used the public toilet in front of her house, and the paradoxical effects of uttering the word rape in the courtroom.

THE DESIRE TO BELIEVE in the redemptive power of exposure is powerful even as we experience its diminishing returns in public life. Think here of the multiple impeachments of Donald Trump, broadcast live on television and radio, which did not cause the widespread outrage that they were supposed to trigger in the minds of everyone who witnessed the scandal of presidential blackmail, corruption, and incitement to commit violence. Consider the far-right mobs that are chanting "Death to the Arabs" and the expulsion of Palestinian families in East Jerusalem on live television.[1] Hindu supremacists in India record their assault on Muslims on cellphones and proudly share them online to become offline heroes.[2] This book has grappled with this *present*, when adapting Bruno Latour, exposure has run out of steam.[3] The covers are off and the will to exclude, marginalize, and brutalize is not concealed but celebrated. So where do we go from here? I have suggested that we need to compose violence in ways that do not simply unmask its brutality, but explain the making, persistence, and consolidation of majorities and minorities within the rule of law, human rights activism, popular politics, and public culture.

This means moving at the edges of exposure, sometimes beside it, showing its limits, never quite abandoning it, staying on the surface to compose objects found within scenes of violence, like the archive, witness, event, law, and activism into a wider map that helps us feel and touch processes of *becoming* majority and minority.

CONCLUSION

MINOR, MINORITIES, MINORITIZATION

A map of the afterlives of political violence as it courses through the courtroom, police documents, activist reports, and mainstream media to form the wounded majority and the killable minority that throbs at the heart of the modern nation state. This special kind of majority and minority are different from the benign entities outlined in graphs, censuses, and civics textbooks, categories tabulated and quantified in surveys and policy documents by experts to make better public policy. Neither are these entities produced through negotiation and debate. Instead, permanent majorities and minorities are forged through violence, both foundational and infrastructural, because they are impediments in the nation-state's fantasy of homogeneity.[4] The genealogy of the creation of murderous majorities and killable minorities leads us to the founding violence of the Western concept of the nation-state itself. What an ethnographic investigation of these categories on the surface of our institutions, our legal system, on the street, in mainstream media, and human rights activism offers is a thread that connects contemporary far-right politics and ethnonationalism across binaries of the North and the South.

The impulse to expose violence is powerful because it is tied closely to notions of justice. Writing about the notion of the nation-state as the telos of history, Joan Scott argues that the "state serves as the last resort for appeals to justice: law, courts, and judges adjudicate—that is they weigh matters of right and wrong, their rulings are equated with the delivery of justice itself. The judgment of history, then, becomes inseparable from the judgments of the designated juridical/legal institutions of the state."[5] The Nuremberg trials and the South African Truth and Reconciliation Commission show the perils of using the law to address forms of violence that are not "ancient hatreds" but are essential to the production and reproduction of the will of the majority that is at the heart of modern politics.[6] If until now exposure was aligned with what Scott calls the judgment of history, then to compose violence is to recognize the limits of the law to undo the relationship between the majority and minority.

By composing violence, we approach the force of violence far beyond the narrow limits of the exceptional and singular Event. To compose violence is to write violence outside the language that sequesters horror and terror to the Global South, places that are forever characterized by state failure, fragility, risk, and primordial attachments; and to interrupt the impulse to read anti-minority violence as a passing aberration within liberal states. Despite Brexit and Trumpism, it is still common to call violence against minorities ethnic violence when it happens in Sri Lanka and Myanmar, but political violence when it is in Washington and London. Instead, by focusing on antiminority violence and its connection to how "a people" are staged, framed, and galvanized[7] by both state and nonstate actors, I offer a way of touching violence that is inextricably connected to the desire of becoming a permanent majority.

The move from exposure to composition is about making a journey in the wake of violence such that we don't already know what we will find at the end. To compose is to step away from the exceptional, the invisible, the mute, the silenced, the unarchived, the undocumented, and the unsayable, and focus instead on the explicit, repeated, and aggregated, on what persists, proliferates, and flourishes in conditions of visibility. This is no doubt risky since violence seems to demand exposure. On the other side of exposure, there may be complicity and silence. Diana Taylor in her analysis of the effects of military violence on the public during Argentina's "Dirty War" describes her efforts "to make visible again, not the invisible or imagined, but that which is clearly there but not allowed to be seen."[8] Taylor analyzes spectacles of violence that blinded the wider population during the Dirty War in Argentina, forcing them to overlook the harm and injury around them. When spectacles of violence do *not* blind but animate the public, allowing large numbers of people to partake in the daily humiliation and subjection of populations designated as minorities, then what violence produces are durable connections between the state, the nation, and the people. Composition is the work that shows how violence is stitched together in the present into a fabric that sustains the making of permanent majorities and minorities.

Minor, minority, and minoritization. Each of these terms seen through a compositional lens is not a frozen, timeless, and singular event with its predictable cast of victims and perpetrators, the monstrous state, and the innocent public, but flows through the surface of our democracies. From the point of view of the minority, impunity is not the rotten core of postcolonial statecraft, the failure of law and order, but is produced in and through the performance of the rule of law. If violence against minorities is construed as a question of illegality, and anti-impunity politics is used to unmask the supremacist state (which is not wearing a mask at all), then we may lose sight of the larger structures of power beyond the scene of violence. The minoritization of Muslims in India did not begin or end with the Gujarat pogrom.[9]

When certain forms of violence seem to occur with predictability of the seasons, an attention to the minor *within* the scene of violence can interrupt the circulation of the major. Take for instance, the so-called minor events that "spark" and "trigger" ethnic violence (called "communal violence" in India). These events carry the potential to unspool the master narrative of primordial hatred. The minor event with its cast of minor characters reveals the relationships between the police, criminals, and mainstream media that compose the conditions of possibility for antiminority violence. One way to follow the minor in the sense in which I have used it in this book is to follow "what everyone knows." What everyone knows and yet does not circulate as public is perhaps one rather rough definition of the minor.

By addressing the explicit nature of the minoritization of Muslims in contemporary India, I join the Indian story to the global present, whether one calls it the rise of right-wing populism, authoritarianism, or fascism across the global North and South. In other words, composition is a tool for our current political conjuncture when hate speech, riots, pogroms, and lynching are the glue that binds the collective into a people. Composition takes us back to those old questions that were supposed to be only the problem of "new states": Who belongs? What brings us together? These questions point us to the attachments that spread outward from scenes of violence that are conventionally framed as breakdown.[10] It is the productivity of violence—its affective, public, and infrastructural aspects—that reorganizes hierarchies, splits the social, and produces new forms of inclusion and exclusion.

The problem of a popular anti-Muslim regime in India is not only that it has subverted the rule of law and constitutional values by demonizing and decimating a large religious minority, but that such an explicitly violent regime is crafting a new kind of people that defies the social divisions of caste and class that should make this people untenable. A steady stream of anti-Muslim images and feelings pass through cellphones, televisions, newspapers, the courtroom, election rallies, and public culture to foster new scenes of solidarity, enmity, and pride for "Hindus." All this is happening in a country of staggering diversity in every aspect of everyday life—language, food, belief, literature, and politics. The Indian case is key to understanding the role of anti-Muslim violence in producing a new political.

Rather than using all our energy to uncover a conspiracy to subjugate and silence minorities (there is no conspiracy because large numbers of people are perfectly willing to say the same in public), this book is a small step in what I hope can be a broader effort to rethink the space of violence within our democracies.[11] Put in the context of India, why and how does anti-Muslim speech, feeling, policy, and media animate millions of people divided by caste, class, region, and language? Especially when large sections of the population are jobless and poor? When encountering mass violence, it is common to ask how ordinary people become murderers overnight. Important as this question may be, I have asked a different question: How does violence compose—a people, a politics, a state, and ultimately a form of life in which a large section of the population enjoys the subjection and humiliation of its neighbors?

Hindu Supremacy: From Scandal to Model

Over the last two decades in India, this form of life, explicit anti-Muslim politics combined with pro-business policies, has transformed from being a scandal into a model. India's current prime minister, Narendra Modi, nearly lost his job in the aftermath of the pogrom and was denied a visa to visit the United States but has transformed his political party into India's "greatest election machine."[12] India has now joined the ranks of right-wing authoritarian democracies like Hungary and Turkey that are characterized by attacks on minorities, journalists, and dissidents and are ruled by a charismatic leader with widespread popular support.

With the benefit of hindsight, it would be easy to say that the pogrom marked the beginning of the end of India's so-called exceptional status as a liberal secular democracy surrounded by ethnic majoritarian states like Sri Lanka and Pakistan. But such an analysis would be unhelpful because Modi's rise over the last two decades is not in opposition to the democratic infrastructure of courts, elections, and the media. Instead, the pogrom in Gujarat was proof that public violence against Muslims would deliver votes, unite a region, and create a new triumphant majority that could withstand unprecedented national and international criticism if it was combined with business-friendly policies, regular elections, and the creation of a continuous threat to the majority from minorities.[13] Perhaps an example here from Gujarat can help us understand how these disparate elements cohere together.

In February 2016, I spent three days in Ahmedabad listening to saffron-clad men and women speaking at the "World Cow Devotee Summit" (*vishwa gau bhakt sammelan*). The audience comprised mostly students from a nearby college. The central message of the summit, repeated by every speaker, performed through song, parable, rhyme, and rousing hate speech was clear: Hindus should overcome their differences (especially caste) and come together as *Hindus*. This pitch for Hindu consolidation was peppered with "facts" about the high birth rate of Muslims and policy suggestions like

C.1 Not a single Hindu nation in the world. A globe representing nations classified according to their religion and a table that shows a zero next to the number of Hindu nations compared to Christian nations (153), Islamic (52), Buddhist (12), and Jewish (1).

death by hanging for those who eat beef. All this material was broadcast live on Sadhana television (a Hindu spiritual television channel) and interspersed with announcements about the Prime Minister Life Insurance and Pension scheme (the minister of state for rural development, Sadhvi Niranjan Jyoti, was one of the speakers). The anchor of the event berated the audience for not understanding the basics of power in a democracy. "Nobody listens to you in a democracy because your vote doesn't count. They know that Hindus don't vote on Hindu lines, but Muslims do. And they only respect those who vote together."

Near the entrance there were posters that said that "everyday eight Hindu women become the victims of love *jihad*[14] in Kerala." Outside the makeshift tent that housed the event, there were booths advertising state-of-the-art biogas plants, and there were representatives from the Hindu Cow Protection Group (Ahmedabad chapter) offering information and membership to those attending the meeting, and another booth was selling cow-based soaps, incense sticks, and finally an organization that ran a cow hostel was giving out flyers. During the event, anti-Muslim sentiment became inseparable from traditions of alternative medicine, an ethics of care for cows, 24/7 cable television, and state welfare schemes. Men and women in saffron came on the stage in front of the television cameras to speak frankly about a new alignment between Hindu supremacy and state power.

The structure of this event, its transmission on television in India and abroad, its publicity in the form of posters and advertisements in Gujarati newspapers, its funding structure that included NRI (non-resident Indian) money, its audience composed of men, women, and young students, and the presence of state officials and welfare schemes suggest that the stability of antiminority politics rests on its ability to attach itself to a range of visible, even hypervisible projects—mega infrastructure, monuments, heritage, conservation, and urban development. This combination of anti-Muslim politics and development is referred to as the "Gujarat model," which depending on whom you are speaking to, can refer to either totalitarian politics or good governance.[15]

A compositional reading of majoritarian world-making helps us understand the heterogeneous and contradictory elements that make antiminority politics popular. Antiminority politics is never simply about destroying a world; it is also about making another one. To understand the second aspect, it is helpful to focus on violence as it is captured and reframed by actors and institutions to construct permanent majorities and minorities. To do this, the task of the analyst is not to unveil, to show why the present situation is inevitable, but rather to draw a map of feelings and words that flow through and between scenes of violence, subjection, pleasure, and solidarity.

Riots, massacres, and pogroms are thus only scene one, act one. When I first reached and worked in relief camps with Muslim survivors in Ahmedabad, the major impulse among scholars, activists, journalists, and nongovernmental organizations was to expose the Hindu nationalist regime's complicity with the mobs that attacked Muslims. There was no dearth of evidence. The massacre was televised. The murder and humiliation of Muslims was celebrated on the streets. Human rights organizations did important work in documenting the horror, showing the complicity of the state and the organized nature of the massacre. In hindsight, it is striking to see the failure of this politics of exposure. Exposing the exceptional in Gujarat did not lead to justice because it did not address the histories, stories, words, feelings, and practices that had made Muslims a publicly killable minority.[16]

The human rights and liberal media's exposure machine to display the horrors of the Gujarat massacre was seized and repurposed by the Hindu nationalists. The head of the Gujarat state and current prime minister of India, Narendra Modi, launched a state-wide public procession to speak out against activists and the opposition's efforts to besmirch the good name of "the people" of Gujarat: a Gujarat Pride Procession. This should have been an early warning for the coming storm. In the 2014 general elections, not a single Muslim was elected from India's largest state, Uttar Pradesh, where they comprise nearly a fifth of the population. The meteoric rise of Hindu supremacy as a mode of governance *beyond* Gujarat is an invitation then to explore the forms, spaces, and affects that bind anti-Muslim violence to liberal democracy. Scenes of dead bodies, looting mobs, grieving survivors, demolished mosques, and overflowing relief camps in 2002 were replaced by state- and capital-sponsored spectacles of a global investment summit in 2003.

Thus, the Gujarat pogrom inaugurated the second flourishing of the Hindu nationalist movement (the first one was in the 1980s), not simply as electoral politics but a grander plan to achieve that old dream, a Hindu *Rashtra* (Hindu Nation). In 2019, the Hindu nationalist regime passed a Citizenship Amendment Act (CAA) that effectively grants citizenship to all persecuted minorities except Muslims. Even though this formal exclusion of Muslims in the government's vision of who can find shelter in India did not go unchallenged, it is nevertheless a key step toward cohering Indian citizenship around the idea of a Hindu state.[17]

Since the former head of the VHP (World Hindu Council), Pravin Togadia, described Gujarat as a laboratory for Hindu nationalism, both critics and supporters have used Gujarat as a metaphor. Critics of Hindu nationalism used the idea of the laboratory to point to the unique and exceptional nature of anti-Muslim sentiment in Gujarat. For the victors, Gujarat 2002 was the awakening, the clarion call that wakened the Hindus, a new era in which the state and the people would join hands to put Muslims in their place as permanent minorities.

With the rise of Narendra Modi beyond Gujarat to the national and international scene (19,000 Modi fans filled Madison Square Garden in 2014), however, the laboratory metaphor has been replaced with the metaphor of the *model*. The Gujarat model, despite its critics, has proliferated across many states in India. The model is an undisguised attempt to meld Hindu supremacy with neoliberal development: to attract global capital,

C.2 Image of Gujarat chief minister Anandiben Patel performing Hindu rituals on the walls of the Sabarmati Riverfront in Ahmedabad.

build mega statues, rewrite history, remake cities, construct riverfronts, and host international investment summits, and at the same time embrace the power of the state to deliver tangible basic goods and services to the poor.[18]

Consider, for example, the walls of the Sabarmati riverfront in Ahmedabad that display scenes of the Gujarat chief minister Anandiben Patel conducting Hindu rituals. This transformation of Gujarat from scandal to model is evidence that public violence against minorities can act like a catalyst to redefine a people, a region, and a politics. To circle back to the key question posed in the introduction: What forms of law, affect, and politics transform violence against minorities into durable forms of rule?

To answer this question, this book has composed objects—witness, archive, victim, and impunity—that are commonly used to unmask violence. Instead of viewing riots and pogroms as pathological social formations characteristic of the primordial hatreds that flow through Indian society, the pogrom and its afterlives is a key moment to grasp the forging of a special kind of majority. This becomes clear when we focus on the mediatory power of political technologies, police archives, courtroom proceedings, mainstream media, and police archives to transform scenes of violence against Muslims into scenes of bonding between people across class, caste, and region.

The legal flows through many of the chapters in this book not as a grand route to return us yet again to the state and its misdemeanors, but rather as a place to understand the intimacy between legal proceduralism, documentation, temporalities, and the making of a killable minority. My point is that the making of the legal is inextricable from the making of the minority, and the law does not merely disenfranchise Muslims but produces them as unreliable, malicious, and sectarian. Anti-impunity activism in the aftermath of the Gujarat pogrom also helps us to see the diminishing returns of legal solutions to political violence against minorities. What do we do when a regime does not bother to conceal its desire to shoot its enemies? At the time of writing this, mainstream political leaders of Kashmir in north India have been under house arrest for over six months and face an indefinite detention. The government has continued to arrest journalists as "terrorists" and has extended its surveillance and detention of Kashmiris. Even the Covid-19 pandemic that has produced such unprecedented suffering and distress across the world has not paused the government's search for enemies. Mainstream television anchors and social media blamed Muslims for *deliberately* spreading the pandemic among the general population by spitting on food and violating the lockdown. #BioJihad was trending on Indian Twitter. Shopkeepers put up posters that announced that they were a "Hindu Fruit Shop." All this is to say that even the most unprecedented global crisis is passing through the binary machine of the majority/minority in India; the fear of Muslims is greater than the fear of an invisible virus that has upended the world.

Nothing however makes the creation of Hindus and Muslims as permanent majorities and minorities in India inevitable. To put it differently, there are many ways to constitute majorities like there are many ways to constitute a people, and Hindu nationalism's remarkable successes in constituting what B. R. Ambedkar called a "communal majority" rests on a vast infrastructure of Hindu supremacist institutions, cultural organizations, and vigilante groups. It also depends on periodic violence to convert the caste and class divisions within Hindu society into a communal and electoral majority.

Ambedkar writes that "Hindu society as such does not exist. It is only a collection of castes. Each caste is conscious of its existence. Its survival is the be-all and end-all of its existence. Castes do not even form a federation. A caste has no feeling that it is affiliated to other castes, except when there is a Hindu-Muslim riot. On all other occasions each caste endeavors to segregate itself and to distinguish itself from other castes."[19] Collective violence against Muslims can temporarily produce a homogenous majority, but as a form of rule it is never stable because it rests on the fiction that Hindu society is undivided and that the meaning and significance of being Hindu is fixed.

The presence and persistence of caste is a major and perhaps the biggest impediment to the making of a Hindu Nation. While secularism can be dismissed as Nehruvian elitism and the language of the English-speaking cultural elites, Hindu supremacists are aware of the vernacular force of caste and the everyday humiliation of lower castes and Dalits (India's "ex-untouchable" caste group). This means that even as they push religious minorities into the spotlight to frame them as internal enemies of the nation, they are equally forceful in attempting to assimilate Dalits and other subaltern castes into the Hindu fold.[20] Their idea of a Hindu nation where Hindus are a permanent communal majority offers no challenge to the forms of brutality that maintain a caste society. This became very clear to me when a member of the Hindu supremacist organization Bajrang Dal, who was always ready to fight Muslims on behalf of Hindus, pointed casually to his Dalit neighbors across the street washing dishes at a public hand pump and said that he would never drink water in their house because they were "dirty."

My emphasis on the making of Muslims into a permanent minority in India may give the impression that the juggernaut of Hindu supremacy rolls without impediment. But that is not the whole story at all. From another angle, Hindu supremacy is in perpetual crisis, seeing enemies and traitors everywhere in the hope that fear will suture together the divisions within Indian society. And it is fearful of forms of belonging that split, fracture, and mold a different people. Consider the recent farmers' struggle in India that led the Hindu nationalist regime to repeal neoliberal farm laws. The farmers did not budge despite arrests and violence and built a coalition across caste and class and region that could not be ignored by the Hindu nationalists, especially not when elections were around the corner. Similarly, the nonviolent protest led by Muslim women against the Citizenship Amendment Act in Delhi's Shaheen Bagh was another attempt by minorities and minor voices in India to occupy public space and make claims to speak in the name of the people. Apart from major events, there are also minor forms of resistance. A Hindu businessman opened his shop to his Muslim neighbors for offering Friday prayers in Gurugram when local Hindu right-wing groups prevented them. After which, Gurugram's oldest *gurudwara* (Sikh place of worship) opened their doors to their Muslim neighbors.[21] These minor acts, voices, and gatherings have the potential to weave together a fabric of life capable of destroying Hindu supremacy.

NOTES

Introduction

1. Avishai Margalit writes that the Russian word *pogrom* meaning destruction is relatively new and has a specific history of anti-Semitic attacks on Jews in Tsarist Europe in the nineteenth and twentieth centuries that included murder, pillage, rape, and looting. It has since then been used to describe public and state-sanctioned attacks on minority ethnic and religious groups across the world. I use the word pogrom to highlight a) the role of state authorities to facilitate a collective public attack on Muslims in Gujarat and b) the role played by pogroms in the making of new nation-states in Europe where Jews would be treated as permanent minorities. See Avishai Margalit, "The Exemplary Pogrom," and Magda Teter, "Rehearsal for Genocide."

2. Human Rights Watch, "We Have No Orders to Save You."

3. Varadarajan, *Gujarat*, 176.

4. Nussbaum, *The Clash Within*; Varadarajan, *Gujarat*.

5. Brass, "Gujarat Pogrom of 2002"; Human Rights Watch, "We Have No Orders to Save You."

6. Nancy Rose Hunt makes a helpful distinction between the idea of a single aftermath versus the many afterlives of violence to track down perceptions, sounds, and the everyday. Afterlives can also be understood as moments of not only bereavement but also rebellion, mourning, struggle, and survival. See Parekh and Kwon, "Introduction: Still Here in the Afterlives," 113.

7. Khetan, "Gujarat 2002."

8. Editors of Communalism Combat, "Genocide Gujarat 2002."

9. Notable exceptions to this framing include Veena Das's *Life and Words*, Gyanendra Pandey's *Routine Violence*, Roma Chatterji and Deepak Mehta's *Living with Violence*,

Pradeep Jeganathan's "After a Riot," and Thomas Blom Hansen's *Law of Force* to name only a few studies on South Asia that reject the framing of violence as exceptional events in order to highlight the everyday, the routine, and the vernacular.

10. Scott, *Refashioning Futures*.

11. Scott, *Refashioning Futures*, 4.

12. I owe this point to Ravi Sundaram.

13. Chatterjee, "Lineages of Political Society."

14. I am indebted to Thushara Hewage for reminding me that the space of the university allows scholars to take risks that are not available to journalists and activists.

15. Hansen, *Law of Force*; Hansen, "Sovereigns beyond the State"; Blight, "American Pogrom."

16. Das, *Life and Words*; Pandey, *Routine Violence*.

17. In no way is this an exhaustive literature review on violence or even anthropological work that exceeds the politics of exposure. I have learned from and build on the extraordinary work of scholars such as Allen Feldman, *Formations of Violence*; Roma Chatterji and Deepak Mehta, *Living with Violence*; Danny Hoffman, *The War Machines*; Achille Mbembe, *On the Postcolony*; and Valentine Daniel's *Charred Lullabies*— to name only a few works that have inspired me.

18. Chatterjee, "Lineages of Political Society," 8.

19. Mamdani, *Neither Settler nor Native*. My idea of "permanent minorities" draws on Mahmood Mamdani's understanding of the making of "permanent minorities" under the colonial state. Building on Mamdani's work on the role of the nation-state in the creation of non-sovereign minorities, I show that ongoing minoritization in democracies can be analyzed ethnographically by tracking the afterlives of violence as it flows through the courts, media, and public culture.

20. Ambedkar, "Communal Deadlock," 377.

21. For a powerful conceptualization of violence in terms of intimacy and fraternity using Indian political thought, see Shruti Kapila, *Violent Fraternity*.

22. Walter Benjamin, "Critique of Violence."

23. Collins and Feldman, "25th Anniversary."

24. Sedgwick and Frank, *Touching Feeling*; Hunt, "Acoustic Register, Tenacious Images, and Congolese Scenes."

25. Hartman, *Scenes of Subjection*, 4.

26. Felski, *Uses of Literature*. See also Felski, *The Limits of Critique*.

27. Coetzee, "Into the Dark Chamber," 364.

28. Levine, *Forms*, 3.

29. Sedgwick and Frank, *Touching Feeling*, 140.

30. Best and Marcus, "Surface Reading."

31. Latour, "Attempt at a 'Compositionist Manifesto,'" 473.

32. Latour, "Attempt at a 'Compositionist Manifesto,'" 474.

33. Latour, "Attempt at a 'Compositionist Manifesto,'" 475.

34. Muecke, "Untitled."

35. Robbins, "Beyond the Suffering Subject."

36. Banerjee, "State (and) Violence."

37. Scott, *Refashioning Futures*, 162.

38. Mbembe and Meintjes, "Necropolitics," 39.

39. Coronil and Skurski, *States of Violence*, 110.

40. Taussig, "Culture of Terror—Space of Death."

41. Mbembe and Meintjes, "Necropolitics."

42. Mufti, *Enlightenment in the Colony*, 2.

43. Asad, *Formations of the Secular*, 7.

44. Reviewers of this book noted that violence against Muslims in India and impunity in the aftermath bear resemblance to historic and contemporary forms of anti-Black violence in the United States and caste violence in India. This is an important question that shows that the question of the minority is inextricable from the forms of violence that produce and reproduce the Black/Muslim/Dalit subject and subjectivity and is foundational to the US and Indian nation-state. The connection between anti-minority violence and the rule of law and state formation does however have different histories and trajectories in the United States and India. For instance, contemporary anti-Black violence and racial terror in the United States are often concentrated in the figure of the police and therefore easier to identify as state violence, whereas pogroms typically involve large sections of "ordinary" people as well as state actors—see Parekh and Kwon, "Introduction." Despite the difference in the forms of violence against different vulnerable groups and their effects on minority communities, I hope that composition as method can be helpful to read and write violence as part of the process of the making of majorities and minorities.

45. Mamdani, *Neither Settler nor Native*.

46. Mahmood, *Religious Difference*, 32.

47. Pandey, *Routine Violence*, 14

48. Hall, *Fateful Triangle*.

49. Asad, *Formations of the Secular*, 165.

50. Asad, "Thought-Provoking Study."

51. See David Scott's "Community, Number, and the Ethos of Democracy" for a wonderful discussion and genealogy of the way in which the logic of number and the inscription of democracy as a "whole new game" in Sri Lanka prepare the path for the inevitable minoritization of Tamils.

52. For a genealogy of the concept of minority in Europe and its Christian history, see Talal Asad, "Muslims as a 'Religious Minority' in Europe," 174–175.

53. Pandey, *Routine Violence*, 10.

54. Hall, *Fateful Triangle*. See also Gyan Pandey, *Routine Violence*.

55. I am indebted to Tridip Suhrud to understand the larger intellectual and political context that undergirds the lack of critique and the worship of consensus in modern Gujarat. See, especially, the online talk "What Have You Done, Mr. Gandhi, https://www.uchicago.in/events/mr-gandhi-what-have-you-done/.

56. Gyan Pandey writes that "it would appear that the notion of a Hindu Rashtra—India as a nation and a Hindu nation, the land of Hindus—was first advanced in the

1920s and the first steps toward the mobilization of Hindus *as a nation* were taken at this time," *Routine Violence*, 106–107.

57. Forbes, *Ras Mala VI*, vii–viii.

58. Isaka, "Gujarati Intellectuals and History Writing in the Colonial Period," 4867.

59. Asif, *The Loss of Hindustan*, 14.

60. Isaka, "Gujarati Intellectuals and History Writing in the Colonial Period."

61. Ghassem-Fachandi, *Pogrom in Gujarat*.

62. Spodek, "From Gandhi to Violence," 787.

63. Spodek, "From Gandhi to Violence," 787.

64. Nandy, "Obituary of a Culture."

65. Suhrud, "Gandhi's Absence," 21.

66. Asif, *The Loss of Hindustan*.

67. Girish Patel also alluded to a broader conservatism that accounts for atrocities against women and Dalits, exclusion of *adivasis* (tribals) and segregation between Hindus and Muslims. He identified the lack of a powerful trade union movement (despite being one of the most industrialized states), the proximity of Gujarat to Pakistan, and the general absence of a large-scale progressive social justice movement as some of the causes for the rise of Hindu nationalism. (Personal communication.)

68. Shah, "The Upsurge in Gujarat," 1437.

69. Shah, "The Upsurge in Gujarat," 1449.

70. For an overview of the transformation of caste and class politics into anti-Muslim violence in Gujarat, see Shani, *Communalism, Caste and Hindu Nationalism*.

71. Berenschot, *Riot Politics*, 10.

72. Bhattacharjee, *Disaster Relief and the RSS*.

73. State of Gujarat v. Girishbhai Revabhai and Others, Sessions Case no. 474/09, Court of the City Sessions Judge Court no. 15, Ahmedabad, October 29, 2010.

74. Felman, *The Juridical Unconscious*.

75. Even as I write this, in the Indian context, the recent Citizenship Amendment Act has perhaps started the slow process of formal disenfranchisement of Muslims. But my point is not to tell the future but show that minoritization is not only about formal rights but also about the right to witness.

76. The limits of framing violence and injustice as the failure of the rule of law also resonates with the way anti-Blackness is woven into the performance of the rule of law in the United States. See Jesse Goldberg's essay that argues anti-Blackness is foundational to the rule of the law in a way such that spectacular and egregious events of anti-Black violence are "not aberrations of the so-called criminal justice system but in fact register the system working as it is constructed to work." Goldberg, "James Baldwin," 521.

77. Wilson, *The Politics of Truth of Reconciliation in South Africa*.

78. Ross, *Bearing Witness*.

79. Felman, *The Juridical Unconscious*.

80. Yngvesson and Coutin, "Backed by Papers," 178.

81. Heyman and Smart, "States and Illegal Practices."

82. Chatterjee, "The Impunity Effect."

83. Agamben, "The State of Exception."

84. Foucault, *Discipline and Punish*.

85. Rutherford, *Laughing at Leviathan*.

86. Hansen and Stepputat, "Sovereignty Revisited," 297.

87. Ghassem-Fachandi, *Pogrom in Gujarat*, 46.

88. Zucchino, *Wilmington's Lie*.

89. Zipperstein, *Pogrom*.

90. Tambiah, *Leveling Crowds*; Brass, *Production of Hindu-Muslim Violence*; Engineer, *Communal Riots*.

91. Chatterjee, "*Bandh* Politics."

92. Krupa and Nugent, *State Theory and Andean Politics*, 5.

93. Mbembe, *On the Postcolony*.

94. Hansen, *The Law of Force*.

95. Krupa and Nugent, *State Theory and Andean Politics*, 11.

96. Blom et al., "Outraged Communities."

97. Butler, *Notes toward a Performative Theory of Assembly*.

98. Sharma, *Final Solution*.

99. Scott, *Refashioning Futures*, 162.

100. Asad, *Formations of the Secular*, 173–174.

101. Scott, *Refashioning Futures*; Pandey, *Routine Violence*.

102. For an overview of majoritarian politics in South Asia, see Mukul Kesavan, "Murderous Majorities."

103. Hewage, "Ideology, Ethnicity, and the Critique of Postconflict"; Scott, *Refashioning Futures*.

104. I am indebted to my reviewers for helping me see the significance of the ease with which the procedures and technicalities associated with due process within a democracy can further harden religious differences and polarize societies into a majority and minority.

105. Abrams, "Notes on the Difficulty of Studying the State."

106. I am indebted to David Nugent for helping me to see this point. See Nugent, "Sacropolitics."

107. Mbembe, *Necropolitics*, 3.

108. Tocqueville and Hacker, *Democracy in America*.

109. Berlant, *The Anatomy of National Fantasy*.

110. Gaonkar, "After the Fictions."

111. Brown, *Politics Out of History*.

112. Lefort and Macey, *Democracy and Political Theory*.

113. Mamdani, *Neither Settler nor Native*.

114. Mazzarella, "The Myth of the Multitude."

115. Derrida, "Archive Fever," 52; Feldman, *Archives of the Insensible*.

Chapter One. A Minor Reading

1. According to a 2011 Indian Readership Survey.

2. A Gujarati word with cognates that can signal depending on the context: chaos, outbreak, rioting, altercation, fighting, turbulence, fracas, tumult, and so on.

3. Breman, *Making and Unmaking.*

4. Ahmedabad, the capital city of the Gujarat, is ostensibly one of the three "dry" states in India. "Dry" means that there is a state prohibition to consume and produce liquor in the state. This is, of course, normative because there is a thriving illegal but licit economy of liquor production, distribution, and consumption in Gujarat.

5. Warner, "Publics and Counterpublics," 12.

6. Taussig, *Defacement.*

7. Warner, "Publics and Counterpublics," 168.

8. Taussig, *Defacement,* 50.

9. Chatterji and Mehta, "Introduction."

10. Grusin, "Radical Mediation."

11. National Human Rights Commission, "Annual Report," 275.

12. Pandey, *Construction of Communalism.*

13. Chatterji and Mehta, *Living with Violence,* 12.

14. See Deepak Mehta's "Writing the Riot: Between the Historiography and Ethnography of Communal Violence in India" in the edited volume *History and the Present* (ed. Partha Chatterjee and Anjan Ghosh) for a discussion of how the historiography of Hindu-Muslim riots excludes voice and assumes a transparent relationship between language and violence.

15. See Richard Fox's critique of communalism as a phenomenon that is particular to India, especially as it usually framed as a pathology peculiar to postcolonial societies or simply a colonial invention to divide and rule ("Communalism and Modernity").

16. Pandey, *Omnibus,* 264.

17. Pandey, *Omnibus,* 32.

18. Baxi, "Adjudicating the Riot."

19. Darshini Mahadevia's article "A City with Many Borders—Beyond Ghettoisation in Ahmedabad" in the book *Indian Cities in Transition* discusses the numerous "borders" in the city that are organized according to "ethnic lines." The area that I discuss in this chapter, the municipal ward, has been designated "mixed" by Mahadevia since both Hindus and Muslims live here in significant numbers.

20. Hansen, "Sovereign beyond the State."

21. For a description of surface reading and its difference from symptomatic forms of reading, see Best and Marcus, "Surface Reading."

22. Gaonkar and Povinelli, "Technologies of Public Forms."

23. Das, "Signature of the State."

Chapter Two. Composing the Archive

1. Grover, "Elusive Quest," 358.
2. Jauregui, *Provisional Authority*.
3. Gupta, *Red Tape*.
4. Gupta, *Red Tape*, 147.
5. Sharma, "State Transparency," 153. Sharma's focus on bureaucratic writing helps us to locate writing practices that erase and obfuscate at the heart of the everyday state. These writing practices are neither exceptional nor a dysfunctional aspect of the modern state.
6. What I call the archive here is more than one hundred police First Information Reports (henceforth FIRs) recorded in the Madhavapura police station between February 28, 2002, when the violence began, and May 12, 2002.
7. Cover, "Foreword."
8. Lynching, hate speech, public humiliation, and so on are some other ways in which this kind of violence circulates in contemporary India. At the time of writing this, parts of mainstream media and Hindu right-wing groups were even suggesting that Muslims were using the coronavirus to infect Hindus as a form of "bio-jihad." In other words, even the global scale and unprecedented actions taken as a response to the virus did not stop it from becoming a part of the majority-minority machine in India.
9. See Hewage, "Event, Archive, Mediation," for a discussion of the limits of ethnographic approaches to the archive.
10. Weld, *Paper Cadavers*, 3.
11. Muecke, "Untitled"; Hunt, "Acoustic Register, Tenacious Images, and Congolese Scenes."
12. Riles, "Infinity within the Brackets," 378.
13. Riles, "Infinity within the Brackets," 378.
14. Stoler, *Along the Archival Grain*.
15. Stoler, "Colonial Archives." See Anjali Arondekar, *For the Record*, for a discussion of the limits of the recovery model of archival research.
16. I want to thank Sarah Muir for emphasizing the discursivity of the so-called nondiscursive riot form within the police reports.
17. For a discussion of the communal riot as a technology of colonial governance see Pandey, *Construction of Communalism*.
18. Das, "Signature of the State."
19. Das, "Signature of the State," 229.
20. Chatterji and Mehta, "Introduction."
21. Taussig, "Culture of Terror."
22. Pandey, *Construction of Communalism*.
23. People's Union for Democratic Rights, "Maaro! Kaapo! Baalo!," 36.
24. Grover, "Elusive Quest," 363.
25. Narrain, "Truth Telling," 217.

26. Narrain, "Truth Telling," 219.

27. Chenoy, Shukla, Subramanian, and Vanaik, "Gujarat Carnage 2002."

28. Brass, "Collective Violence," 324.

29. Ghassem-Fachandi, *Pogrom in Gujarat*, 40, 44.

30. Kapila, *Violent Fraternity*, 265.

31. Derrida, "Structure, Sign and Play," 254.

32. Derrida, "Archive Fever," 54; Feldman, *Archives of the Insensible*.

33. Derrida, *Archive Fever*.

34. Riles, *Documents*, 10.

35. Smith, "Rule-by-Records and Rule-by-Reports," 154.

36. Smith, "Rule-by-Records and Rule-by-Reports," 154.

37. Hull, "Ruled by Records," 503.

Chapter Three. Against the Witness

1. Lazarus-Black and Hirsch, *Contested States*.

2. Mamdani, *Neither Settler nor Native*, 329.

3. Chopra and Jha, *On Their Watch*.

4. Baxi, "Justice Is a Secret," 221.

5. Baxi, "Adjudicating the Riot."

6. Reynolds, "*The Ground of All Making*"; Ross, "Speech and Silence."

7. Felman and Laub, *Testimony*, xvii.

8. Felman and Laub, *Testimony*, 211.

9. I am indebted to Firat Bozcali for helping me clarify this point.

10. For a poignant description of the way human rights trials reproduce forms of violence, see Ram Natarajan, "Courtrooms and Legacies of Violence."

11. Lazarus-Black and Hirsch, *Contested States*.

12. Hong, "Against Witness."

13. Hong, "Against Witness."

14. Vismann, *Files*, 56–57.

15. National Human Rights Commission, "Annual Report," 292.

16. Concerned Citizen's Tribunal, *Crime against Humanity*, 194.

17. People's Union for Democratic Rights, "Maaro! Kaapo! Baalo!," 34.

18. State of Gujarat v. Girishbhai Revabhai and Others, Sessions Case no. 474/09, Court of the City Sessions Judge Court no. 15, Ahmedabad, October 29, 2010.

19. Agamben, *Remnants of Auschwitz*, 120.

20. Meister, *After Evil*.

Chapter Four. Anti-Impunity Activism

1. Nader, *Harmony Ideology*.

2. Moore, "Law and Social Change"; Thomas and Galemba, "Illegal Anthropology."

3. See Shruti Kapila's discussion of the "profoundly intimate nature" of the violence between Hindus and Muslims during the Partition of India and Pakistan in 1947. Kapila's genealogy of the making of Muslims as a minority in India through political violence is crucial to understanding the specific nature of minoritization faced by Muslims in the aftermath of the pogrom in 2002. See Kapila, *Violent Fraternity*, 240.

4. Comaroff and Comaroff, *Law and Disorder*, 78.

5. Over the last decade the state of Gujarat has launched multiple legal investigations against human rights activists for helping Muslim survivors. For more details on how the courts and the police are punishing activists see Lokur, "Condemned by Innuendo."

6. One of the main issues that anti-impunity activism did not address was the question of structural inequality, the causes for Muslim poverty, despite the fact that issues of livelihood and reparation were often the most pressing concerns for survivors. For a discussion of the limits of anti-impunity activism to address structural harm and vulnerability, see Engle, Miller, and Davis, *Anti-Impunity and the Human Rights Agenda*.

7. Shaw and Waldorf, *Localizing Transitional Justice*.

8. Clarke, *Affective Justice*, 15.

9. Shaw and Waldorf, *Localizing Transitional Justice*, 4.

10. See Shruti Kapila's discussion of "fraternal violence" or enmity between neighbors and intimates rather than outsiders/foreigners as foundational to the framing of the political in India. Kapila, "A History of Violence."

11. Human Rights Watch, "Discouraging Dissent."

12. For a discussion of the Supreme Court judgment and the history of the case, see Lokur, "Condemned by Innuendo."

13. Comaroff and Comaroff, *Law and Disorder*.

14. Bornstein and Sharma, "The Righteous and the Rightful."

15. Baxi, "Adjudicating the Riot"; Basu, *Trouble with Marriage*; Berti, "Hostile Witnesses."

16. See chapters 1 and 3 for a discussion of the so-called communal clash that destroyed Abdul's shop in 2011.

17. Shaw and Waldorf, *Localizing Transitional Justice*.

18. Merry, "Postscript."

Chapter Five. Beyond the Unspeakable

1. See Sandhya Fuchs's essay "Strange Bedfellows: On Trauma and Ethnographic Vulnerability" for a discussion of how humor and vulnerability can be the ground for engaging with survivors of violence.

2. Halley, *Split Decisions*, 346.

3. Mookherjee, *Spectral Wound*.

4. Mookherjee, *Spectral Wound*.

5. Das, *Life and Words*.

6. Menon, "Embodying the Self," 101.

7. Taylor, *Disappearing Acts*, 27.

8. Drexler, "History and Liability," 315.

9. Vasa, "2002."

10. Hameed et al., "Survivors Speak."

11. Concerned Citizens Tribunal, *Crime against Humanity*, 43.

12. Hameed et al., "Survivors Speak," 3.

13. Ghassem-Fachandi, *Pogrom in Gujarat*, 66; Sundar, "License to Kill," 80–81.

14. Concerned Citizens Tribunal, *Crime against Humanity*, 133.

15. Hameed et al., "Survivors Speak," 12.

16. Sarkar, "Semiotics of Terror," 2875.

17. Ghassem-Fachandi, *Pogrom in Gujarat*.

18. International Initiative for Justice, "Threatened Existence," 5.

19. International Initiative for Justice, "Threatened Existence," 25.

20. Hameed et al., "Survivors Speak," 33.

21. Baxi, "Adjudicating the Riot."

22. Hameed et al., "Survivors Speak," 9.

23. Kabir, "Double Violation?," 148.

24. Bhasin and Menon, *Borders and Boundaries*, 17.

25. Lok Sabha debate on Gujarat, April 30, 2002, reported on May 1 in *The Hindu*, the *Indian Express*, the *Deccan Herald*, and the *Times of India*.

26. The reference to Delhi 1984 is a debating point to point fingers at the opposition party (the Congress Party), which was in power in Delhi during the anti-Sikh pogrom in 1984.

27. Subsequently Hindu nationalist politicians questioned the existence of this woman, even though eleven people, including family members and others, corroborated the description of her murder given to a citizen's commission by her husband. The perpetrators often destroyed the evidence of sexual violence by burning the bodies, a widespread phenomenon in the Gujarat violence.

28. Khetan, "Gujarat 2002."

29. That conviction has been recently overturned by the Gujarat High Court, acquitting BJP minister Mayaben Kodnani but convicting others.

30. See Veena Das, "Sexual Violence."

31. See Kockelman, "Enclosure and Disclosure."

32. Kabir, "Double Violation?," 161.

33. On August 15, 2022, the Gujarat government released eleven convicts serving life sentences in the Bilkis Bano case under its remission and premature release policy. The convicted men were given sweets and garlanded by their relatives.

Conclusion

1. See David Shulman, "Cracks in the Israeli Consensus," for a description of what is being described as the third intifada in Gaza.

2. Lalwani, "Viral Terror."

3. Latour, "Why Has Critique Run Out of Steam?" See also Gökariksel, "Facing History," for discussion of the risk that exposure may reproduce and even amplify the powers that it seeks to expose.

4. I borrow the idea of permanent majorities from B. R. Ambedkar's distinction between a political majority (variable) and a communal majority (permanent). Ambedkar also points out the necessity of destroying the idea of a permanent communal majority in India to make the rule of majority different from majoritarian rule. See also Mahmood Mamdani's genealogy of the colonial roots of the construction of permanent minorities and Talal Asad's argument about the construction of Muslims as a minority in Europe in the sense that they are considered permanent outsiders to the essence of Europe. Building on these rich genealogical accounts of minorities and majorities, I have outlined an ethnographic route to analyze these categories in the present. See Ambedkar, "Communal Deadlock and a Way to Solve It"; Asad, "Muslims as a Religious Minority in Europe," in *Formations of the Secular*; and Mamdani, *Neither Settler nor Native*.

5. Scott, *On the Judgment of History*, xvii.

6. Pandey, *Routine Violence*.

7. Here I am thinking of the idea that "a people" or "the people" are formed through their invocation and staging in public. See Bosteels, "This People Which Is Not One."

8. Taylor, *Disappearing Acts*.

9. As I write this conclusion, Muslim girls wearing head scarves (hijab) in Karnataka are being disallowed from entering schools and colleges.

10. I follow Stuart Hall in my understanding of the conjuncture. The conjuncture is a moment that is composed of multiple temporalities and competing and contradictory forces that come together to produce a significant shift in what becomes political at any given moment. For my purposes, the current global rise of antiminority politics, especially in the form of global anti-Muslim populism, constitute our present conjuncture. For a discussion of the conjuncture in Stuart Hall, see Hall, *Selected Political Writings*.

11. For an example of such an effort, see The British Academy's report "Violence and Democracy."

12. Jha, *How the BJP Wins*.

13. There is a rich literature that analyzes the transformation of India over the last two decades into a majoritarian democracy. See Jaffrelot, *Modi's India*; Kaur, *Brand New Nation*; and Chatterji, Hansen, and Jaffrelot, *Majoritarian State*.

14. Love *Jihad* refers to the Hindu nationalist myth of a Muslim conspiracy to convert Hindu women by force and through allurement.

15. I am indebted to Hemangini Gupta for helping me to see the importance of neoliberal capitalism in contemporary antiminority projects in India.

16. For a critique of the assumption that LGBTQ visibility naturally leads to rights and justice, see Thomsen, *Visibility Interrupted*.

17. See Chatterjee and Raheja, "India's Citizenship Amendment Act," for an overview and analysis of issues involved in understanding this legislation as part of a longer politics of suspicion around citizenship.

18. Abhishek Anand, Vikas Dimble, and Arvind Subramanian call this modified form of redistributive welfare politics under the Modi regime "New Welfarism." See Anand, Dimble, and Subramanian, "New Welfarism of Modi Govt Represents Distinctive Approach."

19. Ambedkar, "Annihilation of Caste," 19.

20. For a discussion of the relationship between Muslim exclusion and Dalit inclusion to produce a form of authoritarian populism, See Balmurli Natrajan, "Racialization and Ethnicization."

21. As reported by *Scroll.in* on November 18, 2021.

BIBLIOGRAPHY

Abrams, Philip. "Notes on the Difficulty of Studying the State (1977)." *Journal of Historical Sociology* 1, no. 1 (1988): 58–89.

Agamben, Giorgio. *The Remnants of Auschwitz*. New York: Zone Books, 2000.

Agamben, Giorgio. "The State of Exception." In *Politics, Metaphysics, and Death*, edited by Andrew Norris. Durham, NC: Duke University Press, 2005.

Ambedkar, B. R. "The Annihilation of Caste." *Columbia Center for New Media Teaching and Learning*, 1936, https://ccnmtl.columbia.edu/projects/mmt/ambedkar/web/readings/aoc_print_2004.pdf.

Ambedkar, B. R. "Communal Deadlock and a Way to Solve it." In *Dr. Babasaheb Ambedkar Writings and Speeches, Vol. 1*, compiled by Vasant Moon, 355–380. New Delhi: Dr. Ambedkar Foundation, 2014.

Anand, Abhishek, Vikas Dimble, and Arvind Subramanian. "New Welfarism of Modi Govt Represents Distinctive Approach to Redistribution and Inclusion." *The Indian Express*, December 22, 2020, https://indianexpress.com/article/opinion/columns/national-family-health-survey-new-welfarism-of-indias-right-7114104.

Arondekar, Anjali. *For the Record: On Sexuality and the Colonial Archive in India*. Durham, NC: Duke University Press, 2019.

Asad, Talal. *Formations of the Secular: Christianity, Islam, Modernity*. Stanford, CA: Stanford University Press, 2003.

Asad, Talal. "Muslims as a 'Religious Minority' in Europe." In *Formations of the Secular*, 159–180. Stanford, CA: Stanford University Press, 2003.

Asad, Talal. "A Thought-Provoking Study." *The Immanent Frame*, February 11, 2016, https://tif.ssrc.org/2016/02/11/a-thought-provoking-study.

Asif, Manan Ahmed. *The Loss of Hindustan: The Invention of India*. Cambridge, MA: Harvard University Press, 2020.

Banerjee, Prathama. "State (and) Violence." *Seminar*, March 2017, https://www.india-seminar.com/2017/691/691_prathama_banerjee.htm.

Basu, Srimati. *The Trouble with Marriage: Feminists Confront Law and Violence*. Berkeley: University of California Press, 2015.

Baxi, Pratiksha. "Adjudicating the Riot: Communal Violence, Crowds and Public Tranquility in India." In "Riot Discourses," special issue, *Domains* 3 (2007): 66–101.

Baxi, Pratiksha. "Justice Is a Secret: *Compromise* in Rape Trials." *Contributions to Indian Sociology* 44, no. 3 (February 2010): 207–233.

Benjamin, Walter. "Critique of Violence." In *Walter Benjamin: Selected Writings, Volume 1, 1913–1926*, edited by Marcus Bullock and Michael W. Jennings, 236–252. Cambridge, MA: Harvard University Press, 1996.

Berenschot, Ward. *Riot Politics: Hindu-Muslim Violence and the Indian State*. New York: Columbia University Press, 2011.

Berlant, Lauren. *The Anatomy of National Fantasy: Hawthorne, Utopia, and Everyday Life*. Chicago: University of Chicago Press, 1991.

Berti, Daniela. "Hostile Witnesses, Judicial Interactions and Out-of-Court Narratives in a North Indian District Court." *Contributions to Indian Sociology* 44, no. 3 (February 2011): 235–236.

Best, Stephen, and Sharon Marcus. "Surface Reading: An Introduction." *Representations* 108, no. 1 (2009): 1–21.

Bhasin, Kamla, and Ritu Menon. *Borders and Boundaries: Women in India's Partition*. New Delhi: Kali for Women, 2000.

Bhattacharjee, Malini. *Disaster Relief and the RSS: Resurrecting "Religion" Through Humanitarianism*. Thousand Oaks: SAGE Publications, 2019.

Blom, Amélie, Nicolas Jaoul, Thomas Blom Hansen, Nosheen Ali, Ali Riaz, Pierre Centlivres, Lionel Baixas, Charlène Simon, and Christophe Jaffrelot. "'Outraged Communities': Comparative Perspectives on the Politicization of Emotions in South Asia." *South Asia Multidisciplinary Academic Journal* 2 (2008).

Blight, David W. "An American Pogrom." Review of *Wilmington's Lie: The Murderous Coup of 1898 and the Rise of White Supremacy*, by David Zucchino. *New York Review of Books*, November 19, 2020.

Bornstein, Erica, and Aradhana Sharma. "The Righteous and the Rightful: The Technomoral Politics of NGOs, Social Movements, and the State in India." *American Ethnologist* 43, no. 1 (February 2016): 76–90.

Bosteels, Bruno. "Introduction: This People Which Is Not One." In *What Is a People?*, by Alain Badiou, Pierre Bourdieu, Judith Butler, Georges Didi-Huberman, Sadri Khiari, and Jacques Ranciére, 1–20. New York: Columbia University Press, 2016.

Brass, Paul R. "Collective Violence, Human Rights, and the Politics of Curfew." *Journal of Human Rights* 5, no. 3 (2006): 323–340.

Brass, Paul R. "The Gujarat Pogrom of 2002," *Contemporary Conflicts*, March 26, 2004, https://www.almendron.com/tribuna/wp-content/uploads/2019/04/the-gujarat-pogrom-of-2002.pdf.

Brass, Paul R. *The Production of Hindu-Muslim Violence in Contemporary India*. Seattle: University of Washington Press, 2003.

Breman, Jan. *The Making and Unmaking of an Industrial Working Class: Sliding Down the Labour Hierarchy in Ahmedabad, India*. Amsterdam: Amsterdam University Press, 2004.

Brown, Wendy. *Politics Out of History*. Princeton, NJ: Princeton University Press, 2001.

Butler, Judith. *Notes toward a Performative Theory of Assembly*. Cambridge, MA: Harvard University Press, 2015.

Chatterjee, Moyukh. "*Bandh* Politics: Crowds, Spectacular Violence, and Sovereignty in India." *Distinktion: Journal of Social Theory* 17, no. 3 (December 2016): 294–307.

Chatterjee, Moyukh. "The Impunity Effect: Majoritarian Rule, Everyday Legality, and State Formation in India." *American Ethnologist* 44, no. 1 (February 2017): 118–130.

Chatterjee, Partha. "Lineages of Political Society." In *Comparative Political Thought: Theorizing Practices*, edited by Michael Freeden and Andrew Vincent, 80–97. Abingdon-on-Thames: Routledge, 2013.

Chatterjee, Sayantani, and Natasha Raheja. "India's Citizenship Amendment Act (CAA): Citizenship and Belonging in India." *PoLAR: Political and Legal Anthropology Review*, September 7, 2020.

Chatterji, Angana, Thomas Blom Hansen, and Christophe Jaffrelot. *Majoritarian State: How Hindu Nationalism Is Changing India*. Oxford: Oxford University Press, 2019.

Chatterji, Roma, and Deepak Mehta. "Introduction." *Domains* 3 (February 2007): 11–16.

Chatterji, Roma, and Deepak Mehta. *Living with Violence: An Anthropology of Events and Everyday Life*. London: Routledge India, 2007.

Chenoy, Dr. Kamal Mitra, S. P. Shukla, K. S. Subramanian, and Achin Vanaik. "Gujarat Carnage 2002: A Report to the Nation." *Outlook India*, April 11, 2002.

Chopra, Surabhi, and Prita Jha. *On Their Watch: Mass Violence and State Apathy in India, Examining the Record*. Gurgaon: Three Essays Collective, 2014.

Clarke, Kamari Maxine. *Affective Justice: The International Criminal Court and the Pan-Africanist Pushback*. Durham, NC: Duke University Press, 2019.

Coetzee, John Maxwell. "Into the Dark Chamber: The Writer and the South African State." In *Doubling the Point: Essays and Interviews*, 361–368. Cambridge, MA: Harvard University Press, 1992.

Collins, John, and Allan Feldman. "The 25th Anniversary of 'On Cultural Anesthesia: From Desert Storm to Rodney King.'" *American Ethnologist*, April 25, 2020.

Comaroff, Jean, and John L. Comaroff. *Law and Disorder in the Postcolony*. Chicago: University of Chicago Press, 2006.

Concerned Citizens Tribunal. *Crime against Humanity: An Inquiry into the Carnage in Gujarat, Lists of Incidents and Evidence, Volume 1.* Citizens for Justice and Peace, 2002.

Coronil, Fernando, and Julie Skurski. *States of Violence.* Ann Arbor: University of Michigan Press, 2006.

Cover, Robert M. "Foreword: Nomos and Narrative." *Harvard Law Review* 97, no. 4 (2013): 4–68.

Daniel, E. Valentine. *Charred Lullabies: Chapters in an Anthropography of Violence.* Princeton, NJ: Princeton University Press, 1996.

Das, Veena. "Sexual Violence, Discursive Formations and the State." *Economic and Political Weekly* 31, no. 35/37 (September 1996): 2411–2423.

Das, Veena. "The Signature of the State: The Paradox of Illegibility." In *Anthropology in the Margins of the State*, edited by Deborah Poole, 225–252. Santa Fe, NM: School for Advanced Research, 2004.

Das, Veena. *Life and Words: Violence and the Descent into the Ordinary.* Berkeley: University of California Press, 2006.

Derrida, Jacques. *Archive Fever: A Freudian Impression.* Chicago: University of Chicago Press, 1996.

Derrida, Jacques. "Archive Fever in South Africa." In *Refiguring the Archive*, edited by Carolyn Hamilton, Verne Harris, Michéle Pickover, Graeme Reid, Razia Saleh, and Jane Taylor, 54. Cape Town: David Philip, 2002.

Derrida, Jacques. "Structure, Sign, and Play in the Discourse of the Human Sciences." In *The Structuralist Controversy: The Languages of Criticism and the Sciences of Man*, edited by Richard Macksey and Eugenio Donato, 247–265. Baltimore, MD: The Johns Hopkins University Press, 1970.

Drexler, Elizabeth. "History and Liability in Aceh, Indonesia: Single Bad Guys and Convergent Narratives." *American Ethnologist* 33, no. 3 (August 2006): 313–326.

Editors of Communalism Combat. "Genocide Gujarat 2002." *Communalism Combat*, March–April 2002.

Engineer, Asghar Ali. *Communal Riots in Post-Independence India.* Hyderabad: Sangam Books, 1984.

Engle, Karen, Zinaida Miller, and Denys Mathias Davis. *Anti-Impunity and the Human Rights Agenda.* Cambridge: Cambridge University Press, 2016.

Feldman, Allen. *Archives of the Insensible: Of War, Photopolitics, and Dead Memory.* Chicago: University of Chicago Press, 2015.

Feldman, Allen. *Formations of Violence: The Narrative of the Body and Political Terror in Northern Ireland.* Chicago: University of Chicago Press, 2008.

Felman, Shoshana. *The Juridical Unconscious: Trials and Traumas in the Twentieth Century.* Cambridge, MA: Harvard University Press, 2002.

Felman, Shoshana, and Dori Laub. *Testimony: Crises of Witnessing in Literature, Psychoanalysis, and History.* New York: Routledge, 1992.

Felski, Rita. *The Limits of Critique.* Chicago: University of Chicago Press, 2015.

Felski, Rita. *Uses of Literature*. Hoboken, NJ: Wiley-Blackwell, 2008.

Forbes, Alexander Kinloch. *Ras Mala Vı: Or Hindoo Annals of The Province of Goozerat, In Western India (1856)*. Whitefish: Kessinger Publishing, 2010.

Foucault, Michel. *Discipline and Punish: The Birth of the Prison*. New York: Vintage Books, 1977.

Fox, Richard. "Communalism and Modernity." In *Contesting the Nation: Religion, Community, and the Politics of Democracy in India*, edited by David Ludden, 235–249. Philadelphia: University of Pennsylvania Press, 1996.

Fuchs, Sandhya. "Strange Bedfellows: On Trauma and Ethnographic Vulnerability." Allegra Lab, July 2021, https://allegralaboratory.net/strange-bedfellows-on -trauma-and-ethnographic-vulnerability/.

Gandhi, M. K. *An Autobiography, Or the Story of My Experiments with Truth*. Ahmedabad: Navajivan Publishing House, 1992.

Gaonkar, Dilip. "After the Fictions: Notes towards a Phenomenology of the Multitude." *E-Flux*, October 2014, https://www.e-flux.com/journal/58/61187/after -the-fictions-notes-towards-a-phenomenology-of-the-multitude.

Gaonkar, Dilip Parameshwar, and Elizabeth A Povinelli. "Technologies of Public Forms: Circulation, Transfiguration, Recognition." *Public Culture* 15, no. 3 (Autumn 2003): 385–397.

Ghassem-Fachandi, Parvis. *Pogrom in Gujarat: Hindu Nationalism and Anti-Muslim Violence in India*. Princeton, NJ: Princeton University Press, 2012.

Gökariksel, Saygun. "Facing History: Sovereignty and the Spectacles of Justice and Violence in Poland's Capitalist Democracy." *Comparative Studies in Society and History* 61, no. 1 (January 2019): 111–114.

Goldberg, Jesse A. "James Baldwin and the Anti-Black Force of Law: On Excessive Violence and Exceeding Violence." *Public Culture* 31, no. 3 (September 2019): 521–538.

Grover, Vrinda. "The Elusive Quest for Justice: Delhi 1984 to Gujarat 2002." In *Gujarat: The Making of a Tragedy*, edited by Siddharth Varadarajan, 356–388. Delhi: Penguin Books India, 2002.

Grusin, Richard. "Radical Mediation." *Critical Inquiry* 42, no. 1 (Autumn 2015): 124–148.

Gupta, Akhil. *Red Tape: Bureaucracy, Structural Violence, and Poverty in India*. Durham, NC: Duke University Press, 2012.

Hall, Stuart. *The Fateful Triangle: Race, Ethnicity, Nation*. Cambridge, MA: Harvard University Press, 2017.

Hall, Stuart. *Selected Political Writings: The Great Moving Right Show and Other Essays*. Edited by Sally Davison, David Featherstone, Michael Rustin, and Bill Schwarz. Durham, NC: Duke University Press, 2017.

Halley, Janet. *Split Decisions: How and Why to Take a Break from Feminism*. Princeton, NJ: Princeton University Press, 2008.

Hameed, Syeda, Ruth Manorama, Sheba George, Farah Naqvi, and Mari Thekaekara. "The Survivors Speak." *Outlook India*, April 16, 2002.

Hansen, Thomas Blom. *The Law of Force: The Violent Heart of Indian Politics*. New Delhi: Aleph Books, 2021.

Hansen, Thomas Blom. "Sovereigns beyond the State: On Legality and Authority in Urban India." In *Sovereign Bodies*, edited by Thomas Blom Hansen and Finn Stepputat. Princeton, NJ: Princeton University Press, 2005.

Hansen, Thomas Blom, and Finn Stepputat. "Sovereignty Revisited." *Annual Review of Anthropology* 35 (September 2006): 295–315.

Hartman, Saidiya V. *Scenes of Subjection: Terror, Slavery, and Self-Making in Nineteenth-Century America*. Oxford: Oxford University Press, 1997.

Hewage, Thushara. "Event, Archive, Mediation: Sri Lanka's 1971 Insurrection and the Political Stakes of Fieldwork." *Comparative Studies in Society and History* 62, no. 1 (January 2020): 186–217.

Hewage, Thushara. "Ideology, Ethnicity, and the Critique of the Postconflict in Sri Lanka." *Society for Cultural Anthropology*, March 24, 2014, https://culanth.org/fieldsights/ideology-ethnicity-and-the-critique-of-postconflict-in-sri-lanka.

Heyman, Josiah, and Alan Smart. "States and Illegal Practices: An Overview." In *States and Illegal Practices*, 1–24. New York: Bloomsbury Academic, 1990.

Hoffman, Danny. *The War Machines: Young Men and Violence in Sierra Leone and Liberia*. Durham, NC: Duke University Press, 2011.

Hong, Cathy Park. "Against Witness: Paul Celan, Doris Salcedo, and Memory in the Internet Age." *Poetry Magazine*, May 1, 2015.

Hull, Matthew S. "Ruled by Records: The Expropriation of Land and the Misappropriation of Lists in Islamabad." *American Ethnologist* 35, no. 4 (November 2008): 501–518.

Human Rights Watch. "Discouraging Dissent: Intimidation and Harassment of Witnesses, Human Rights Activists, and Lawyers Pursuing Accountability for the 2002 Communal Violence in Gujarat." *Human Rights Watch*, September 2004.

Human Rights Watch. "'We Have No Orders to Save You': State Participation and Complicity in Communal Violence." *Human Rights Watch*, April 30, 2002.

Hunt, Nancy Rose. "An Acoustic Register, Tenacious Images, and Congolese Scenes of Rape and Repetition." *Cultural Anthropology* 23, no. 2 (2008): 220–253.

International Initiative for Justice in Gujarat. "Threatened Existence: A Feminist Analysis of the Genocide in Gujarat." *OnlineVolunteers.org*, December 2003.

Isaka, Riho. "Gujarati Intellectuals and History Writing in the Colonial Period." *Economic and Political Weekly* 37 no. 48 (November 30–December 6, 2002): 4867–4872.

Jaffrelot, Christophe. *Modi's India: Hindu Nationalism and the Rise of Ethnic Democracy*. Princeton, NJ: Princeton University Press, 2021.

Jauregui, Beatrice. *Provisional Authority: Police, Order, and Security in India*. Chicago: University of Chicago Press, 2016.

Jeganathan, Pradeep. "After a Riot: Anthropological Locations of Violence in an Urban Sri Lankan Community." PhD diss., University of Chicago, 1997.

Jha, Prashant. *How the BJP Wins: Inside India's Greatest Election Machine*. New Delhi: Juggernaut Books, 2017.

Kabir, Ananya Jahanara. "Double Violation? (Not) Talking about Sexual Violence in Contemporary South Asia." In *Feminism, Literature and Rape Narratives*, edited by Sorcha Gunne and Zoe Brigley Thompson, 146–163. Abingdon-upon-Thames: Routledge, 2011.

Kapila, Shruti. "A History of Violence." *Modern Intellectual History* 7, no. 2 (August 2010): 437–457.

Kapila, Shruti. *Violent Fraternity: Indian Political Thought in the Global Age*. Princeton, NJ: Princeton University Press, 2021.

Kaur, Ravinder. *Brand New Nation*. Stanford, CA: Stanford University Press, 2020.

Kesavan, Mukul. "Murderous Majorities." *New York Review of Books*, January 18, 2018.

Khetan, Ashish. "Gujarat 2002: The Truth in the Words of the Men Who Did It." *Tehelka*, October 26, 2007.

Kockelman, Paul. "Enclosure and Disclosure." *Public Culture* 19, no. 2 (April 2007): 303–305.

Krupa, Christopher, and David Nugent. *State Theory and Andean Politics: New Approaches to the Study of Rule*. Philadelphia: University of Pennsylvania Press, 2015.

Lalwani, Vijayta. "Viral Terror: Why the Perpetrators of the Anti-Muslim Assaults Are Broadcasting Their Own Crimes." *Scroll.in*, September 2, 2021.

Latour, Bruno. "An Attempt at a 'Compositionist Manifesto.'" *New Literary History* 41, no. 3 (Summer 2010): 471–490.

Latour, Bruno. "Why Has Critique Run Out of Steam? From Matters of Fact to Matters of Concern." *Critical Inquiry* 30, no. 2 (Winter 2004): 225–248.

Lazarus-Black, Mindie, and Susan F. Hirsch. *Contested States: Law, Hegemony, and Resistance, After the Law*. New York: Routledge, 1994.

Lefort, Claude, and David Macey. *Democracy and Political Theory*. Cambridge: Polity Press, 1988.

Levine, Caroline. *Forms: Whole, Rhythm, Hierarchy, Network*. Princeton, NJ: Princeton University Press, 2017.

Lokur, Madan B. "Condemned by Innuendo: Some Questions on the SC Order That Led to Teesta Setalvad's Arrest." Wire.in, June 28, 2022.

Mahadevia, Darshini. "A City with Many Borders—Beyond Ghettoisation in Ahmedabad." In *Indian Cities in Transition*, edited by Annapurna Shaw, 341–389. New Delhi: Orient BlackSwan, 2007.

Mahmood, Saba. *Religious Difference in a Secular Age: A Minority Report*. Princeton, NJ: Princeton University Press, 2015.

Mamdani, Mahmood. *Neither Settler nor Native: The Making and Unmaking of Permanent Minorities*. Cambridge, MA: Harvard University Press, 2020.

Margalit, Avishai. "The Exemplary Pogrom." *New York Review of Books*, May 23, 2019.

Mazzarella, William. "The Myth of the Multitude, or, Who's Afraid of the Crowd?" *Critical Inquiry* 36, no. 4 (Summer 2010): 697–727.

Mbembe, Achille. *Necropolitics*. Durham, NC: Duke University Press, 2019.

Mbembe, Achille. "The Power of the Archive and Its Limits." In *Refiguring the Archive*, edited by Carolyn Hamilton, Verne Harris, Michéle Pickover, Graeme Reid, Razia Saleh, and Jane Taylor, 19–27. Berlin: Springer, 2002.

Mbembe, J-A. *On the Postcolony*. Berkeley: University of California Press, 2001.

Mbembe, J-A, and Libby Meintjes. "Necropolitics." *Public Culture* 15, no. 1 (Winter 2003): 11–40.

Mehta, Deepak. "Writing the Riot: Between the Historiography and Ethnography of Communal Violence in India." In *History and the Present*, edited by Partha Chatterjee and Anjan Ghosh, 149–174. New Delhi: Permanent Black, 2002.

Mehta, Nalin, and Mona G Mehta. *Gujarat beyond Gandhi: Identity, Society and Conflict*. Abingdon-on-Thames: Routledge, 2013.

Meister, Robert. *After Evil: A Politics of Human Rights*. New York: Columbia University Press, 2012.

Menon, Nivedita. "Embodying the Self: Feminism, Sexual Violence and the Law." In *Subaltern Studies XI: Community, Gender, and Violence*, edited by Partha Chatterjee and Pradeep Jeganathan, 66–106. New Delhi: Permanent Black, 2000.

Merry, Sally Engle. "Postscript to Legal Vernacularization and Transitional Culture: The Ka Ho'okolokolonui Kanaka Maoli, Hawai'i." *PoLAR: Political and Legal Anthropology Review*, virtual edition (2016), https://polarjournal .org/2016-virtual-edition-sally-engle-merry/.

Mookherjee, Nayanika. *The Spectral Wound: Sexual Violence, Public Memories, and the Bangladesh War of 1971*. Durham, NC: Duke University Press, 2015.

Moore, Sally Falk. "Law and Social Change: Semi-Autonomous Social Field as an Appropriate Subject of Study." *Law and Society Review* 7, no. 4 (Summer 1973): 719–746.

Muecke, Stephen. "Untitled." In *The Hundreds*, edited by Lauren Berlant and Kathleen Stewart. Durham, NC: Duke University Press, 2019.

Mufti, Aamir. *Enlightenment in the Colony: The Jewish Question and the Crisis of Postcolonial Culture*. Princeton, NJ: Princeton University Press, 2007.

Nader, Laura. *Harmony Ideology: Justice and Control in a Mountain Zapotec Village*. Stanford, CA: Stanford University Press, 1990.

Nandy, Ashis. "Obituary of a Culture." *Seminar*, May 2002, https://www.india -seminar.com/2002/513/513%20ashis%20nandy.htm.

Narrain, Arvind. "Truth Telling, Gujarat and the Law." *Sarai Reader 04: Crisis/Media* (2004): 207–217.

Natarajan, Ram. "Courtrooms and Legacies of Violence." *LASA Forum* XLIV, no. 3 (Summer 2013): 24–25, https://forum.lasaweb.org/files/vol44-issue3/Debates-3.pdf.

National Human Rights Commission, "Annual Report, 2001–2002." *National Human Rights Commission*, accessed August 6, 2022, https://nhrc.nic.in/sites/default /files/Annual%20Report%202001-2002.pdf.

Natrajan, Balmurli. "Racialization and Ethnicization: Hindutva Hegemony and Caste." *Ethnic and Racial Justice* 45, no. 2 (2022): 298–318.

Nugent, David. "Sacropolitics." In *The Encrypted State: Delusion and Displacement in the Peruvian Andes*, 28–49. Stanford, CA: Stanford University Press, 2019.

Nussbaum, Martha Craven, *The Clash Within: Democracy, Religious Violence, and India's Future*. Cambridge, MA: Harvard University Press, 2007.

Pandey, Gyanendra. *The Construction of Communalism in Colonial North India*. New Delhi: Oxford University Press, 2012.

Pandey, Gyanendra. *The Gyanendra Pandey Omnibus: The Ascendancy of the Congress in Uttar Pradesh; The Construction of Communalism in Colonial North India; Remembering Partition*. New Delhi: Oxford University Press, 2008.

Pandey, Gyanendra. *Routine Violence: Nations, Fragments, Histories*. Stanford, CA: Stanford University Press, 2006.

Parekh, Shanti, and Jong Bum Kwon. "Introduction: Still Here in the Afterlives." *American Ethnologist* 47, no. 2 (May 2020): 110–120.

Patel, Girish. "Narendra Modi's One-Day Cricket: What and Why?" *Economic and Political Weekly* 37, no. 48 (November 30–December 6, 2002): 4826–4837.

People's Union for Democratic Rights. "'Maaro! Kaapo! Baalo!': State, Society, and Communalism in Gujarat." May 2002, https://www.onlinevolunteers.org/gujarat/reports/pudr/pdf/full_report.pdf.

Reynolds, Pamela. *"The Ground of All Making:" State Violence, the Family, and Political Activists*. Pretoria: Co-operative Research Programme on Marriage and Family Life (Human Sciences Research), 1995.

Riles, Annelise. *Documents: Artifacts of Modern Knowledge*. Ann Arbor: University of Michigan Press, 2006.

Riles, Annelise. "Infinity within the Brackets." *American Ethnologist* 25, no. 3 (August 1998): 378–398.

Robbins, Joel. "Beyond the Suffering Subject: Toward an Anthropology of the Good." *Journal of the Royal Anthropological Institute* 19, no. 3 (August 2013): 447–462.

Ross, Fiona C. *Bearing Witness: Women and the Truth and Reconciliation Commission in South Africa*. London: Pluto Press, 2003.

Ross, Fiona C. "Speech and Silence: Women's Testimony in the First Five Weeks of Public Hearings of the South African Truth and Reconciliation Commission." In *Remaking a World*, edited by Veena Das, Arthur Kleinman, Margaret Lock, Mamphela Ramphele, and Pamela Reynolds. Berkeley: University of California Press, 2001.

Rutherford, Danilyn. *Laughing at Leviathan: Sovereignty and Audience in West Papua*. Chicago: University of Chicago Press, 2012.

Sarkar, Tanika. "Semiotics of Terror: Muslim Children and Women in Hindu Rashtra." *Economic and Political Weekly* 37, no. 28 (July 2002): 2872–2876.

Scott, David. "Community, Number, and the Ethos of Democracy." In *Refashioning Futures: Criticism after Postcoloniality*, 158–189. Princeton, NJ: Princeton University Press, 1999.

Scott, David. *Refashioning Futures: Criticism after Postcoloniality*. Princeton, NJ: Princeton University Press, 1999.

Scott, Joan Wallach. *On the Judgment of History*. New York: Columbia University Press, 2020.

Sedgwick, Eve Kosofsky, and Adam Frank. *Touching Feeling: Affect, Pedagogy, Performativity, Series Q*. Durham, NC: Duke University Press, 2003.

Shah, Ghanshyam. "The Upsurge in Gujarat." *Economic and Political Weekly* 9, no. 32/34 (August 1974): 1429–1454.

Shani, Ornit. *Communalism, Caste, and Hindu Nationalism: The Violence in Gujarat*. Cambridge: Cambridge University Press, 2007.

Sharma, Aradhana. "State Transparency after the Neoliberal Turn: The Politics, Limits, and Paradoxes of India's Right to Information Law." *PoLAR: Political and Legal Anthropology Review* 36, no. 2 (October 2013): 308–325.

Sharma, Rakesh, director. *Final Solution*. 2004. 2 hrs., 31 min. https://vimeo.com /329340055.

Shaw, Rosalind, and Lars Waldorf. *Localizing Transitional Justice*. Stanford, CA: Stanford University Press, 2010.

Shulman, David. "Cracks in the Israeli Consensus." *New York Review of Books*, July 1, 2021.

Smith, Richard Saumarez. "Rule-by-Records and Rule-by-Reports: Complementary Aspects of the British Imperial Rule of Law." *Contributions to Indian Sociology* 19, no. 1 (January 1985): 153–176.

Spodek, Howard. "From Gandhi to Violence: Ahmedabad's 1985 Riots in Historical Perspective." *Modern Asian Studies* 23, no. 4 (1989): 765–795.

Stoler, Ann Laura. *Along the Archival Grain: Epistemic Anxieties and Colonial Common Sense*. Princeton, NJ: Princeton University Press, 2010.

Stoler, Ann Laura. "Colonial Archives and the Arts of Governance." *Archival Science* 2 (March 2002): 87–109.

Suhrud, Tridip. "Gandhi's Absence." *India International Centre Quarterly* 37, no. 2 (Autumn 2010): 16–25.

Sundar, Nandini. "A License to Kill: Patterns of Violence in Gujarat." In *Gujarat: The Making of a Tragedy*, edited by Siddharth Varadarajan, 75–134. Delhi: Penguin Books India, 2002.

Tambiah, Stanley Jeyaraja. *Leveling Crowds: Ethnonationalist Conflicts and Collective Violence in South Asia*. Berkeley: University of California Press, 1996.

Taussig, Michael. "Culture of Terror—Space of Death. Roger Casement's Putumayo Report and the Explanation of Torture." *Comparative Studies in Society and History* 26, no. 3 (July 1984): 467–497.

Taussig, Michael T. *Defacement: Public Secrecy and the Labor of the Negative*. Stanford, CA: Stanford University Press, 1999.

Taylor, Diana. *Disappearing Acts: Spectacles of Gender and Nationalism in Argentina's Dirty War*. Durham, NC: Duke University Press, 1997.

Teter, Magda. "Rehearsal for Genocide." *New York Review of Books*, June 9, 2022.

Thomas, Kedron, and Rebecca B. Galemba. "Illegal Anthropology: An Introduction." *PoLAR: Political and Legal Anthropology Review* 36, no. 2 (October 2013): 211–214.

Thomsen, Carly. *Visibility Interrupted: Queer Life and the Politics of Unbecoming.* Minneapolis: University of Minnesota Press, 2021.

Tocqueville, Alexis de, and Andrew Hacker. *Democracy in America.* New York: Washington Square Press, 1964.

Varadarajan, Siddharth. *Gujarat: The Making of a Tragedy.* Delhi: Penguin Books India, 2002.

Vasa, Samia. "2002: A Reading Appeal." *Differences* 30, no. 3 (December 2019): 34–62.

"Violence and Democracy." *The British Academy,* September 2019.

Vismann, Cornelia. *Files: Law and Media Technology.* Stanford, CA: Stanford University Press, 2008.

Warner, Michael. "Publics and Counterpublics." *Public Culture* 14, no. 1 (Winter 2001): 49–90.

Weld, Kirsten. *Paper Cadavers: The Archives of Dictatorship in Guatemala, American Encounters/Global Interactions.* Durham, NC: Duke University Press, 2014.

Wilson, Richard. *The Politics of Truth and Reconciliation in South Africa: Legitimizing the Post-Apartheid State.* Cambridge: Cambridge University Press, 2001.

Yngvesson, Barbara, and Susan Coutin. "Backed by Papers: Undoing Persons, Histories, and Return." *American Ethnologist* 33, no. 2 (May 2006): 177–190.

Zipperstein, Steven. *Pogrom: Kishinev and the Tilt of History.* New York: Liveright, 2019.

Zucchino, David. *Wilmington's Lie: The Murderous Coup of 1898 and the Rise of White Supremacy.* New York: Atlantic Monthly, 2020.

INDEX

Mamdani, Mahmood, 140n19, 149n4

Mander, Harsh, 98

media: anti-Muslim politics and, 130–131, 136, 145n8; minor reading and, 38–42, 49–50; pogrom and, 5–6, 11, 14, 27–28; sexual violence and, 109–113, 123; split along linguistic lines, 100–102

Mehta, Deepak, 41

Menon, Nivedita, 110

minor: in the archive, 58–59, 75; concept of, 14, 129–130; as a form of reading, 30–31, 38–39, 53–55; media reports of, 49–50; police reports of, 43–45; as public, 52–55; within modernity, 12–13

minoritization: across world contexts, 12–13; activism and, 90, 95; composition and, 129–130, 141n51, 142n75, 147n3 (chap. 4); racialization of Muslims and, 16; role of trials in, 80–84, 102; sexual violence and, 109–114

Modi, Narendra, 4, 60, 94, 97, 100–101, 131, 134

Mookherjee, Nayanika, 110

Mufti, Aamir, 12

Muslims: beyond victimhood, 71–73, 103–105, 124–126; the communal riot and, 38, 40–43; in the laboratory of Hindu nationalism, 16–21; a minor public created by, 52–54; pogrom against, 1–5, 25–26; in the police archive, 68–71; status in Europe, 12–13; as witnesses, 85–87

nation (nation-state): fantasies of, 28–29; pogroms in, 7; sexual violence and, 123–124; the space of minorities within, 12–14; violence against minorities in, 11–12, 128–129, 137. *See also* Hindu Nation

National Human Rights Commission (NHRC), 40, 89, 102

Pandey, Gyanendra, 41, 42, 62. *See also* riot

Patel, Girish, 19, 142n67

performative: crowd politics as, 24–25

"the people": activism defined as against, 100–103; democracy and, 28–29, 149n7; produced by violence, 6–9, 11–13, 24–25

pogrom: as composing the political, 23–26; democracy and, 28–29; as experiment in Gujarat, 16–19; to make permanent majority and minority, 7–9; public nature of, 2–5

police: legal infrastructure and, 21–23; local strongmen and, 36–37; narrative of the riot produced by, 43–45; partisan nature of, 2, 57–58. *See also* First Information Report

politics of exposure: definition and limits of, 5–6; moving at the edges of, 127–129, 140n17; sexual violence and, 107–111; witnessing and, 81–84; working beyond, 8–10, 24–25

postcolonial: democracy and, 26–30; statecraft and, 11–12; theory's approach to, 5–7, 23–26; violence and, 24–28. *See also* colonial

publics: anti-Muslim violence and, 38–39; exposure and, 6–7

repetition: activists use of, 93–94; concept of, 14, 31, 58–60; police reports and, 60–63, 65, 68; sexual violence and, 110, 123

Right to Information, 59

riot: caste and, 136–137; circulation in newspapers, 45–47; colonial narrative of, 42–43, 62; Gujarat government and, 40–41; minor reading of, 38–40; police narrative of, 43–45; spontaneous theory of, 24, 40, 60–66

rule of law: anti-impunity and, 32, 99–100, 106; democracy and, 26–27; majorities and minorities composed by, 127–130, 141n44; procedural activism linked to, 94–96; the space of violence in, 5–8

Scott, David, 5, 27, 141n51

Sedgwick, Eve, 10

sexual violence: absence and presence of, 109–111; composing a new scene of, 124–126; framed as exaggeration, 122; the nation and, 123; as unspeakable, 112–116

Shah, Ghanshyam, 19

Sharma, Aradhana, 101

sovereignty: dispersed in India, 48; popular and, 25–26, 29; postcolonial and, 11, 23–24

Spodek, Howard, 19

state: anti-minority violence sanctioned by, 6–7, 9–10; majorities and minorities in, 4–5, 11–14; nonstate actors and, 7, 12; theories of, 24

Supreme Court of India, 5, 57, 70, 98, 101, 102

Taussig, Michael, 39

Taylor, Diana, 129

testimony: activist approach to, 94, 101–102; the crisis of, 81–84; dismissal of, 14, 21, 32, 88–89; excluded from police

reports, 65; sexual violence and, 107–114. *See also* witnessing

time: *bandh* and, 66–68; riot narrative and, 61–62; witnessing and, 97–98, 103–105

unspeakable. *See* sexual violence

visibility: the politics of, 124; sexual violence and, 33, 109–110; violence and, 11, 129. *See also* bandh; pogrom

Warner, Michael, 39

Weld, Kristin, 59

witnessing: the crisis of, 81–84; individual versus collective, 85; the limits of, 91–92; Muslims excluded from, 21–22, 66, 79–80, 85, 87–88; the space of, 86–90. *See also* testimony

World Hindu Council (VHP): Gujarat and, 16–17, 70–71; pogrom and, 3–4; shutdown declared by, 66–67

9 781478 019664